SO-AUX-590

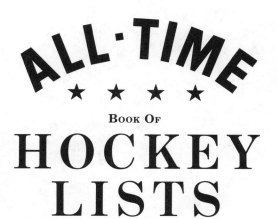

ALL·TIME

★ ★ ★ ★

BOOK OF

HOCKEY
LISTS

STAN & SHIRLEY FISCHLER'S

ALL·TIME

★ ★ ★ ★

BOOK OF

HOCKEY LISTS

Complete With Stories, Trivia & Humor
- ★ The All-Time Toughest Players
- ★ The All-Time Best Playoff Performers
- ★ The 15 Best Clutch Scorers
- ★ The Best Draft Picks
  and much, much more...

Stan Fischler, author of the best-selling **Bad Boys**

Copyright © 1993 Stan Fischler

All rights reserved. No part of this publication may be reproduced or transmitted in any form or by any means, or stored in a data base and retrieval system, without the prior written permission of the publisher.

First published in 1993 by
McGraw-Hill Ryerson Limited
300 Water Street
Whitby, Ontario, Canada
L1N 9B6

Canadian Cataloguing in Publication Data

Fischler, Stan 1932 —
      The all-time book of hockey lists

ISBN 0-07-551503-2

1. Hockey — Miscellanea. 2. Hockey — Anecdotes.
3. National Hockey League — Miscellanea.
I. Fischler, Shirley. II. Title.

GV847.F58 1992   796.962   C92—095511-8

Cover Design: Jim Williamson, Shaftesbury Books.
Photographs: Fischler Hockey, NYC.

This book was produced for McGraw-Hill Ryerson by Shaftesbury Books, a member of the Warwick Publishing Group, Toronto, Canada.

ACKNOWLEDGEMENTS

Since this is a book of lists, it's only appropriate that one of the most important be the list of those whose contributions helped make this book possible.

For starters there was Don Broad of McGraw-Hill Ryerson and Don Loney of Word Guild Publishing Services, who both saw the potential in the germ of an idea and encouraged us to develop it into a book.

Many friends and journalistic colleagues provided ideas and for their contributions we offer unlimited thanks. These include: Chris Loman, John Halligan, Kevin Snow, Steve Hutcheon, Ashley Scharge, Eric Servetah, Matt Messina, Scott Tracht, Brian McDonough, Keith Drabik, Anthony Hamilton, Kevin Mackay, Kevin Friedman, Lal Puri, Jim Ramsey, Dan Carle, Rob Daly, Alan Rozinsky, Joel Bergman, Kevin Allenspach, Sean Farrell, Susan Bloom, Richard Middleton, Diane Gerace, Dean Kovacevic, Al Goldfarb, Randy Hu, Thomas Losier, Lisa Chenier, Sandra MacPherson, Mary McCarthy, Joe Plozarv, David Margalit, George Eliou, Michael Lieberman, James Robinson, Steve Karasik, Rita Gelman, Todd Diamond.

★ CONTENTS ★

THE FOUR CURSES THAT PREVENT THE RANGERS FROM WINNING THE CUP

1. *Red Dutton*
   Former owner of the New York Americans, he claimed the Rangers lobbied to prevent his club from moving to nearby Brooklyn and so followed up with an eternal curse.

2. *The Mortgage-Burning Curse*
   On February 1, 1941, Ranger owners John Kilpatrick, Bernard Gimbel and Stanton Griffis gathered for a photo opportunity. They also owned the old Madison Square Garden, and their $3 million mortgage had just been paid off. Since they had the Stanley Cup in their possession, the three men burned the mortgage inside the trophy. By desecrating the most revered trophy in professional sports by using it as an oven, the Rangers were cursed to never win the Cup again.

3. *The Penn Station Massacre*
   When built in 1910, Pennsylvania Station was considered one of the architectural wonders of the world, located at 33rd Street and 7th Avenue in Manhattan. In the mid-1960s, owners of Madison Square Garden decided that a new arena should be constructed and, incredibly, chose the Penn Station site. To the horror of New Yorkers, the station was razed and in its place rose one of the truly ugly arenas of all time. City preservationists were so appalled they created a Landmarks Commission to prevent such atrocities from being repeated and, of course, put a curse on the Rangers.

4. *The Denis Potvin Curse*
   Although he was the most competent defenseman in the New York metropolitan area, Potvin was constantly reviled by Ranger fans, even after his retirement. Of course, this prompted Denis to voodoo the Broadway Blueshirts.

THREE DUMB PLACES TO PUT HOCKEY TEAMS

1. *Macon, Georgia, brief home of the Macon Whoopees*
    In the 1974 season, somebody got the bright idea that there was a hockey boom in Georgia just because the Atlanta Flames were in the NHL. Thus, a minor league team was put in Macon and given the unlikely name of the Whoopees. The team folded before the season was over.

2. *Oakland, California, home of the Oakland Seals*
    When the NHL expanded from six to 12 teams in 1967, it wanted a team in San Francisco. There was only one problem: The new arena happened to be across the bay in Oakland. Folks stayed away by the millions. By 1976, the NHL got the message and moved the franchise to Cleveland.

3. *Cherry Hill, New Jersey, home of the New Jersey Knights*
    When the WHA's New York Golden Blades failed at Madison Square Garden they moved to Cherry Hill, and became known as the New Jersey Knights. Unfortunately, their home rink, the Cherry Hill Arena, was somewhat smaller than a medium-sized barn. Another problem was that the ice developed a little ski slope near the center face-off circle which was disconcerting to back-skaters. Otherwise, it was a hell of a rink.

THE TWO FLUKIEST CUP-WINNING GOALS INVOLVING THE CANADIENS AND THE RED WINGS

In the early 1950s, the Canadiens and the Red Wings had the best teams in hockey, and when they met in the playoffs the series usually went to the limit, as was the case in 1954. The series reached its seventh-game climax on April 16, 1954 at Olympia Stadium in Detroit.

The Canadiens scored first on a goal by Floyd Curry, but Red Kelly tied it in the second period for the Red Wings. Nobody scored in the third period, setting the stage for climactic sudden death, which turned out to be exceedingly anti-climactic.

Just after the four-minute mark, Detroit moved into Montreal territory. The Canadiens seemed to have the situation well in hand

This man may not look significant to you, but he sure is meaningful to Detroit Red Wings historians. The very under rated Jimmy Skinner coached the Motor City sextet to Detroit's last Stanley Cup in 1954-55.

when Red Wings left wing Tony Leswick — who scored only 10 goals all season — released a seemingly ineffectual shot at goalie Gerry McNeil. "Hard Luck" Gerry, who had made a brief comeback with the Canadiens, appeared to have it in hand when defenseman Doug Harvey attempted to knock it down. Harvey managed to get only a piece of the puck and it caromed off his left gauntlet and into the net behind the startled McNeil at 4:29 of overtime.

In the 1966 Canadiens-Red Wings Cup Final, the Habs led three games to two entering game six. The match, played at Olympia Stadium, was tied 2-2 at the end of three periods. John Ferguson, who played left wing for the Canadiens at the time, explained exactly what happened.

"The ending was as weird and anti-climatic as you could imagine, but we decided to take it anyway. Naturally, with the packed house in the Olympia roaring like mad from the opening face-off in sudden-death, the Red Wings came out with a bang, but Gump [Canadiens goaltender Gump Worsley] defused them right off the bat, and we settled down to what could have been a long and excruciating game.

"It was anything but. Not long after the two-minute mark, Toe [Canadiens Coach Blake] sent the Pocket Rocket, Dave Balon and Jim Roberts out for a shift. We won the puck in their end and it went to Balon. He tried to get it to Henri, but Richard was pulled down as he was heading for the net. Meanwhile, the puck was at the Pocket's skates as he was careening toward Red Wing goalie Roger Crozier. It was like a guy being in the middle of a bobsled track as a bobsled is coming at him.

"Anyway, Richard kept sliding and sliding and sliding at Crozier until, the next thing we knew, he slid right into the net, with the puck and Crozier. The goal judge had no choice but to hit the red light because the puck had crossed the line. Meanwhile, Toe was watching the whole proceeding from the bench and the minute he saw the light flash, he yelled up and down the bench, 'GET OUT ON THE ICE! GET OUT ON THE ICE!' So, we tumbled off the bench and headed for Richard, as if we had won the Stanley Cup.

"Now here's the weird part. The goal probably should have been disallowed by referee Frank Udvari, because Richard must have slid a good fifteen yards down the ice and into the net with it. If he had disallowed it we wouldn't have had a gripe, I assure you. At least, not a legitimate one.

"Blake was thinking of the theory of the fait accompli. That is, if we jumped the hell over the boards in a hurry and made it seem like it was legit, maybe Udvari would swallow his whistle. If he swallowed it long enough, well, that would make it legal, wouldn't it?

"Toe was exactly right. Udvari seemed stunned by the whole business, really mummified. He looked around momentarily and did nothing in the way of even attempting to wave off the goal. Gump said he had his eyes on Crozier, who just stood at the net in a state of shock, looking at the puck, thinking, 'What the hell is this?' The Red Wings were as much in a trance as Udvari, and by now we knew that it had counted, and the celebration was begun in earnest."

THE TEN BEST GENERAL MANAGERS

1. *Frank Selke, Jr.*
   At the close of World War II, Selke moved from the Toronto Maple Leafs to the Montreal Canadiens and constructed the foremost dynasty the sport has ever known.

2. *Conn Smythe*
   Selke's mentor, Smythe organized the original New York Rangers and then built the Maple Leafs into a winner. His single best accomplishment was the design of the Stanley Cup winners in 1947, 1948, 1949 and 1951.

3. *Glen Sather*
   Slats took over a young team under difficult circumstances and produced five Stanley Cup winners (1984, 1985, 1987, 1988 and 1990) in a remarkably short time. His club continued winning despite the losses of Wayne Gretzky and Paul Coffey.

4. *Bill Torrey*
   At a time when the World Hockey Association had decimated NHL rosters, the New York Islanders were born. Torrey patiently built the club around brilliant draft choices such as Denis Potvin and Bryan Trottier and produced four straight Stanley Cup championships in 1980, 1981, 1982 and 1983.

5. *Sam Pollock*
   Although the Canadiens' machine might have faltered after Selke's retirement, Pollock redesigned it, assuring that Montreal would remain a major contender throughout the 1970s.

6. *Tommy Gorman*
   Never has a general manager been successful with more different teams than Gorman. He managed three different Stanley Cup winners (the Ottawa Senators, Chicago Blackhawks and Montreal Canadiens) and also provided the New York Americans with a few moments of glory.

7. *Jack Adams*
   The Detroit Red Wings during the 1930s and 1940s were among the NHL's most consistently dominating teams. Adams created the farm system that delivered Gordie Howe et. al. to Detroit.

8. *Art Ross*
   One of the most creative hockey thinkers, Ross developed an endless series of aces, starting with Eddie shore and culminating with the Boston Bruins' renowned Kraut Line.

9. *Tommy Ivan*
   A crumbling Chicago Blackhawks franchise was saved from complete destruction by Ivan, who rebuilt a farm system that led to the Windy City's last Stanley Cup in 1961.

10. *Punch Imlach*
   The retirement of Conn Smythe left the Maple Leafs aimlessly fluttering in the 1950s. Imlach resurrected the club and produced four Stanley Cup winners in the 1960s.

The Ten Best Coaches

1. *Hector "Toe" Blake*
   It is enough to say that Blake guided the Montreal Canadiens to eight Stanley Cup championships, including a run of five straight Cups from 1956 through 1960.

2. *Hap Day*
   The man who engineered the greatest comeback in Cup history (1942 vs. the Detroit Red Wings), Day coached five Stanley Cup winners, including a then unprecedented run of three in a row in the late 1940s.

3. *Scotty Bowman*
   Brilliant at times, Bowman won four straight Stanley Cups (1976, 1977, 1978, 1979) for the Canadiens. While he momentarily lost his spark in Buffalo, Bowman hadn't lost his skill. He heavily influenced Bob Johnson's 1991 Pittsburgh Stanley Cup win, but Bowman's most arresting accomplishment was his masterful handling of the Penguins in their 1992 playoff conquest.

4. *Glen Sather*
   Both general manager and coach of the Oilers, he had to develop a youthful corps including Wayne Gretzky, Mark Messier and Kevin Lowe. He did it to the tune of four Stanley Cups in five years (1984-1988), before turning the coaching reins over to John Muckler.

5. *Al Arbour*

    When Arbour took control of the Islanders, they were at a subterranean level. He patiently guided them to a position of prominence and respect while winning four Stanley Cups.

6. *Lester Patrick*

    Patrick's name is etched on three Stanley Cups; once with the Victoria Cougars and twice with the New York Rangers. He was innovative and inspiring.

7. *Dick Irvin*

    After coaching the Maple Leafs to a Stanley Cup in 1932, Irvin later won three Cups for the Canadiens. He harnessed Maurice Richard and produced magnificently exciting "firewagon style" teams.

8. *Tommy Ivan*

    When Jack Adams molded the Red Wings into a contender in the early 1950s, it was Ivan who masterminded Stanley Cup wins in 1950, 1952 and 1954.

9. *Punch Imlach*

    Carrying the dual title of general manager and coach never bothered Imlach. Apart from his four Stanley Cups, he demonstrated that older skaters could be resurrected and turned into big winners.

10. *Anatoli Tarasov*

    The "Father of Soviet hockey," Tarasov demonstrated to the North Americans that European creativity could be used to an advantage in the NHL. His teams were among the first to persuade both Canadian and American fans that the best hockey was not necessarily played on this side of the Atlantic.

THE ELEVEN BEST DEFENSIVE DEFENSEMEN

1. *Doug Harvey*
    Best known for his total ice generalship, Harvey was the centerpiece of the successful Montreal Canadiens club in the 1950s because of his defensive excellence.

2. *Tim Horton*
    Somewhat less creative than Harvey, Horton nevertheless patrolled his side with diligence and power during the Toronto Maple Leafs' golden era of the early 1960s.

3. *Eddie Shore*
    Shore's versatility as a rushing defenseman with the Boston Bruins was complemented by his crunching play behind the blue line.

Aubrey ("Dit") Clapper played his first 10 years in the NHL as a star forward and the last 10 as a top flight defenseman — all with the Boston Bruins.

4. *Ching Johnson*
   The towering New York Ranger spent little time rushing when there was so much bodychecking to be done. He was the best Manhattan has ever seen.

5. *Hap Day*
   A vastly superior intelligence (in relation to most other defensmen) gave Day an advantage, which he exploited to the fullest on the Maple Leafs of the early 1930s.

6. *Emile Bouchard*
   Overshadowed by the Punch Line, "Butch" Bouchard was the first of the grand post-World War II Canadiens defensemen who made life infinitely easier for Vezina-winner Bill Durnan.

7. *Jack Stewart*
   There were few stronger men or more emphatic hitters or diligent defense players than Black Jack. The Detroit Red Wings would have been impotent without him.

8. *Dit Clapper*
   The Bruins defense centered around this stately and thoughtful athlete who was quite willing to use his body as well as his head.

9. *Jim Thomson*
   When the Toronto Maple Leafs won three straight Stanley Cups (1947, 1948 and 1949), the defense of Thomson and Gus Mortson was impenetrable. Mortson rushed more often. Thomson quietly did the defensive work.

10. *Allan Stanley*
    The quintessential defensive defenseman, Stanley was pivotal — along with Horton — during the Toronto reign of the early 1960s.

11. *Rod Langway*
    When Langway moved to Washington in September 1982, the Caps were a dismal non-playoff team. Rod became the defensive anchor, leader and sparkplug. While he was at it, Langway also won a pair of Norris Trophies; the last defensive defenseman to accomplish that feat.

THE SIX BEST LITTLE MEN IN HOCKEY

1. *King Clancy*
   There was never a more resilient defenseman who managed to distill humor and courage with his artistry. The fact that he never won a fight during his lengthy NHL career never tempered his pugnacity.

2. *Roy "Shrimp" Worters*
   Altough the goaltending theory has always been "the more net filled the better," Worters amply demonstrated that a tiny man with catlike moves could play as well — or better — than the best of the big ones. Worters was the best of the little men and, in the opinion of some, the best of them all.

3. *Ted Lindsay*
   Notorious for the vicious use of his stick, Lindsay nevertheless could handle his dukes and was one of the most dangerous offensive left wings in the game. "Old Scarface" was never hampered by his size.

4. *Henri Richard*
   A French-Canadian version of Lindsay, The Pocket Rocket was every inch as tough as his brother Maurice and a remarkable playmaker to boot. The mind boggles at the thought of Henri Richard's ability inside Jean Beliveau's body.

5. *Yvan Cournoyer*
   Never one to raise a fist in anger, The Roadrunner exploited speed above all. His pacifism never proved to be a deterrent.

6. *Denis Savard*
   The slippery little Montreal Canadiens centerman has survived 12 seasons in the NHL. He broke in with the Blackhawks, and in 1987-88 scored 44 goals and added 87 assists. As recently as 1991-1992, Savard was good enough to rank second on the Canadiens' scoring list.

THE TEN BEST ARENAS OF ALL TIME

1. *Boston Garden*
   Reeking with nostalgia and never modernized in the manner of the Montreal Forum or Maple Leaf Gardens, The Bruins' home is the Ebbets Field of the NHL. Sadly, the Gah-den will soon be demolished and replaced by a modern arena.

2. *Maple Leaf Gardens*
   The jewel of Canadian arenas. "The House That Conn Smythe Built" has retained much of the flavour of opening night in 1931. Introduction of organ music diminished its appeal.

3. *Montreal Forum*
   Like its Toronto counterpart, the Forum remains a shrine. Its lobby is graced with bronze castings of the Canadiens' top heroes. Post-World War II improvements have not hurt a bit, and like Boston Garden, it will soon be history.

4. *Chicago Stadium*
   Despite its location in a seedy part of Chicago, the Stadium — like Boston Garden — oozes with history. The cavernous interior still echoes with cheers for the Bentleys and Bobby Hull. It, too, will make way for Chicago Stadium II.

5. *Detroit Olympia*
   Gone but not forgotten, the showcase theater for Gordie Howe, Ted Lindsay and Sid Abel, the Olympia is also remembered for Pete Cusimano, the octopus thrower at Red Wings games.

6. *Old Madison Square Garden*
   Located at Forty-Ninth street and Eighth Avenue, a block from Times Square, the Old Garden had terrible sight lines from the side balcony, but a magnificent ambience that made one love New York hockey.

7. *Quebec Colisee*
   "The House That Jean Beliveau Built" has been enlarged since Le Gros Bill played for the Quebec (Junior) Citadels. The 100 percent Gallic crowd is unmatched throughout the league.

8. *St. Louis Arena*
   Although it has been completely refurbished, the St. Louis Arena dates back to 1929. Its loaf-of-bread roof and two adjacent towers make it unique.

9. *The Spectrum*
   One of the least flawed hockey rinks, the Spectrum is equally appreciated by fans and media alike. There is good seating for all. Rooters, they say, will boo the loser of a wheelchair race. Soon they will be doing it at Spectrum II across the road.

10. *Nassau Coliseum*
    Not only are even the cheapest seats obstruction free but the sky boxes and press areas provide the best views possible. Built in 1970, the Coliseum has the good feel of a venerable arena.

THE TEN BEST REFEREES OF ALL TIME
(OR IS THIS A CONTRADICTION IN TERMS)

1. *John Ashley*
   Invariably calm and always in complete command of the ice, Ashley was both distinguished in appearance and performance. The fact that he had been a professional defenseman for many years added to his insights.

2. *Mickey Ion*
   When this man told a colleague, in a rink jammed with 15,000 frenzied fans, "There are only two sane people here — you and me," he was betraying the good sense that made him a superior whistle blower.

3. *Bill Chadwick*
   Although sightless in one eye, this courageous New York-born official saw more than most refs. He backed down from no one and made some of the most difficult calls in crucial situations of any of his ilk. When Detroit owner Jim Norris tried to have him fired, it proved he was a winner.

4. *King Clancy*

   Like Ashley, Clancy had been a defenseman who could translate his playing experience to hockey's penal system. His ebullience and humour gave him an edge over his more serious brethren.

5. *Bobby Hewitson*

   Remarkably, this gentle perceptive fellow was the sports editor of the *Toronto Telegram*, while a full time NHL referee. He handled a whistle as well as he did an editorial pencil.

6. *Red Storey*

   A flame-haired, towering referee, Storey imparted his knowledge as both a football and hockey star to the rinks. Controversial to a fault, Storey cut short his own career, resigning in protest over an "off the record" critique made by NHL president Clarence Campbell.

7. *Jack Mehlenbacher*

   The sleeper of referees, Mehlenbacher did his job so quietly, effectively and efficiently, that no one ever bothered to acknowledge his superiority, other than the players, who respected his work.

8. *Mike Rodden*

   It is no accident that this referee from hockey's earlier era is in the Hall Of Fame. Curiously, Rodden, like Bobby Hewitson, also was a sports editor for a Canadian daily.

9. *Cooper Smeaton*

   An official who saw things clearly and saw them whole, Smeaton was so distinguished a referee that he was later named a trustee of the Stanley Cup.

10. *Frank Udvari*

    An absolutely abysmal (even he'd admit that) referee in his early years, Udvari eventually ripened into one of the very best. Long after his retirement, he was summoned from the stands at Nassau Coliseum to pinch-hit for an injured referee. Although wearing his suit pants and borrowed skates, Udvari proceeded to officiate one of the best games ever in the building.

The Short A — Z Hockey List

Abbreviations

AHAUS	- Amateur Hockey Association of the US
ECHL	- East Coast Hockey League
IHL	- International Hockey League
NHA	- National Hockey Association
NHL	- National Hockey League
OHA	- Ontario Hockey Association
OHL	- Ontario Hockey League
QMJHL	- Quebec Major Junior Hockey League
USHL	- United States Hockey League
WCHL	- Western Canadian Hockey League
WHA	- World Hockey Association
WHL	- World Hockey League.

Animals

"Pete," the Pittsburgh Penguin mascot (a real Penguin, naturally), who died of pneumonia; the bat that invaded Buffalo's War Memorial Auditorium during the playoff game between the Sabres and the Philadelphia Flyers; Greg Polis stickhandling with his dog; Roger Neilson and his dog practicing patience in the crease; Don Cherry and his famous dog Blue (who appeared with him regularly on TV); the skating bear in the Old Madison Square Garden; the octopi that brothers Jerry and Pete Cusimano used to toss on the ice at old Detroit Olympia Stadium, in order to bring playoff luck to the Red Wings; all the poor dead chickens sacrificed to the ice of various arenas throughout the NHL when fans wanted to comment on the lack of nerve of a hated opponent.

Black Stars

Grant Fuhr, Willie O'Ree, Alton White, Mike Marson, Bill Riley, Herb and Ossie Carnegie, Manny McIntyre, Dale Craigwell, Claude Vilgrain, Eldon "Pokey" Reddick, Graeme Townshend and Reggie Savage.

Crossbar

The goalie's best friend when you are beaten by a shot and it deflects off the crossbar and caroms away from the net; in Ron Hextall's case, the crossbar is more useful for him to repeatedly hit with his stick before each face-off.

Deke

Usually a head move employed to beat a player and continue on with the puck.

Dive

What Mike Keenan accuses Mario Lemieux of doing too often.

Equipment

Lightweight padding, plastic helmet, clamp skates, strap-on blades, Achilles tendon guards, ballistic nylon (replaced leather on boots), plastic boot, shinguards, elbow pads, shoulder guards, gloves, molded mask, plastic mask, birdcage wire mask attached to a helmet, face-shield (plexi-glass), football helmet (protection around jaw) pants, neck collars.

Fans

Paul Gardella, the man who did not miss a Rangers' home game for 970 dates epitomizes hockey aficionados. Also movie actor Jim Belushi and television star George Wendt for their Chicago Blackhawks; and the fan who jumped on the ice and challenged the Sabres' bench in Quebec and proceeded to get a beating.

Faceoff

The dropping of a puck to start play at the beginning of each period; face-offs are more important when taken in your own zone. A good win can lead to a goal or help kill a penalty. Ask Adam Oates, who took a shot right off the face-off and scored a game winning overtime goal in 1992.

Goal Crease

Supposedly the ice moat protecting goalies from the rest of the world. The NHL has changed the rules on the goal crease in terms of what can and can't be done in this blue semi-circle.

Hat Trick

This is accomplished when a player scores three goals in a game and results in the throwing of hats onto the ice by a crowd. A "pure" hat trick occurs when three goals are uninterrupted by any other goals. A "natural" hat trick occurs when the player gets three goals in one period.

Iron Men

Murray Murdoch, Glenn Hall, Gordie Howe, Andy van

Hellemond, Ray Bourque, Johnny Wilson, Garry Unger, Steve Larmer.

Jumping

A player jumps trying to get out of the way of a puck or when jumping over the boards onto the ice. Sometimes players will jump in the air to catch a high shot. The ultimate jump is the one that follows a goal being scored.

Kingston

Kingston, Ontario was the site of a game played by the Royal Canadian Rifles in 1885. It is believed to be the site of the first organized ice hockey league.

Kicking

This action is legal only when the puck is kicked ahead to a teammate or anywhere on the ice surface, except when being used to score a goal. If a player kicks the puck into the net or re-deflects a shot with his feet into the cage, the goal will be disallowed. Players like Peter Zezel are adept at using their feet in action. "Skate Kicking" — when one player kicks a another player's skates out from under him — is considered one of the dirtiest moves, and a penalty can result if the perpetrator is caught.

Luck (Charms and Superstitions)

Andy Bathgate would tap both goalposts with his stick; Frank Paice, former trainer of the Rangers, and general manager Emile Francis would return to the same restaurant on the road if the team won there. The "magic" drink concoted by Gene Leone that led the Rangers on a winning streak in 1950-51. The Philadelphia Flyers and Kate Smith singing her rendition of "God Bless America": It had a 49 wins, six losses and one tie record up to the start of the 1977-78. The Blackhawks and the "Curse of Pete Muldoon." The Rangers and their 52-year curse. Claude Lemieux is always the last person on the ice at the end of practice, in order to put the puck in the opposition's goal.

Minor Leagues

American, International, East Coast and Central, among the best known. From the past, Pacific Coast, United States and Eastern Leagues, to name a few.

Native North Americans

Jimmy Jamieson, Fred Sasakamoose, Jim Neilson, George Armstrong, Henry Boucha, Gary Sargent, Reggie Leach, Stan Jonathan, Gino Odjick, Jamie Leach.

Organists

Gladys Goodding, the organist for the Rangers at the old Madison Square Garden, would play different songs for different teams. Norm Wullen played "Sabre Dance" in Buffalo. John Kiley, at the Boston Garden in 1940, played "Paree." Al Melgard of Chicago who retired after the 1974-75 season, was the "dean" of organists and the first ever recognized sports organist. Norm Kramer, who played "St. Louis Blues" to usher the Blues onto the ice and introduced "When the Saints (Blues) Go Marching In" after a Blues' goal. Vic Hadfield's slapshot caromed up the arena walls and hit a key on the organ; the key broke and the organ played continuously. The organist in the film "Slap Shot" was knocked out when hit in the head with a puck. Next game, the organist wore a helmet.

Penalty Box

Otherwise known as the sin bin. Before expansion (1967) arenas had only one box and penalized players sat next to each other on the same bench.

Pulling the Goalie

Usually done late in the game by a team which is down by one or two goals. By pulling the goalie, the team can put an extra offensive player on the ice. Also done when a delayed penalty is called. Some coaches will pull the goalie despite even a three-goal deficit!

Quebec

Home at various times to the Bulldogs, Citadelles, Remparts and, most recently, Les Nordiques.

Referees

Mickey Ion refereed for 30 years and was enshrined in the Hall of Fame. He would tell new referees, "From the time the game starts until it ends, you and I are the only sane ones in the rink." One of the earliest referees was Fred C. Waghorne, who officiated for more than 50 years and 2,000 games; Bill Chadwick introduced hand signals to signify penalties.

Ragging

Retaining the puck with expert stickhandling, a'la Edgar Laprade, Wayne Gretzky, Jean Beliveau, Pete Morin, et. al.

Screen Shot

A puck that is shot through a maze of players often unseen by the goalie to the very end. Many screened shots are carefully executed from the point. Others happen by accident when the puck's trajectory has been changed by a deflection.

Slapshot

A shot made by bringing the stick at least to waist height or above and then downswinging golf style directly behind the puck; Brett Hull has the most frightening slapshot today. Ray Bourque has the most accurate slapshot.

Trainers

Frank Paice, who served the New York Rangers from 1947-48 through 1977-78, had one of the longest runs of any trainers. Among the more popular contemporary trainers is Bearcat Murray of the Calgary Flames. In recent years trainers have become more sophisticated in their treatment than in the early days.

Udvari

One of the few referees ever inducted into the Hockey Hall of Fame, Frank Udvari was a less effective official than his Hall of Fame induction would indicate. However, unlike some of his more outspoken contemporaries of the late Fifties and early Sixties, Udvari was more of an establishment official who, unlike Dalt MacArthur, Eddie Powers or Red Storey, rarely criticized NHL management. An inferior referee when he began his career, Udvari did mature into a competent whistleblower. He was rewarded for his efforts after retirement when the NHL named him one of the league's supervisors of officials.

Vezina Trophy

Leo Dandurand, Louis Letourneau and Joe Cattarinich, former owners of the Montreal Canadiens, presented a trophy to the National Hockey League in 1926-27 in memory of Georges Vezina, the Canadiens' outstanding goaltender who collapsed during an NHL game on November 28, 1925 and died of tuberculosis a few months later. The first winner was George Hainsworth of the Canadiens, Vezina's successor, who won the trophy three years in a row — 1927, 1928 and 1929. Another Canadiens' ace, Bill Durnan, won the Vezina four years in a row from 1944 through 1947. Durnan also won the prize in 1949 and 1950. Still another Montreal goaltender, Jacques Plante, set a record, winning the Vezina in five consecutive seasons from 1956 through 1960, and again in 1962. Plante shared the Vezina with teammate Glenn Hall of St. Louis in 1969.

Ward

Center Ron Ward is probably the strangest feast-or-famine story in modern hockey. After playing briefly with the Toronto Maple Leafs (no goals scored), and one full season with the Vancouver Canucks (two goals scored), Ward jumped to the New York Raiders of the WHA and started making up for lost time.

By season's end, Ron had racked up 51 goals and finished second among league scorers. Yet before the following season ended, Ward had been traded three times, and Ward ultimately wound up in Cleveland.

Xenophobia

"Fear and hatred of strangers or foreigners..."
— Websters Dictionary

This could easily describe the NHL immediately following World War II and up to expansion in 1967-68. For years the only non-Canadian playing was Tommy Williams. The Duluth, Minnesota native was with the Bruins from 1961-62 through 1968-69. He then trekked to Minnesota, California for the Seals and a couple of seasons with the New England Whalers of the WHA before finishing his career with the Caps.

Today's NHL has no room for xenophobia. For instance, in the 1992 Entry Draft, the number two choice in the first round (picked by Ottawa) was a Russian, Alexei Yashin. There are now hundreds of non-Canadians playing the NHL circuit. Who'da' thunk it, 20 years ago!

Young

At one point (1962-63), defenseman Howie Young was regarded as the wildest, if not the toughest, skater in the NHL. He collected 273 penalty minutes that year, breaking Lou Fontinato's seven-year record and put the fear of God in many a foe. A super skater and hard shot, Young found inflammatory beverages more a challenge than his opponents. He played five seasons for the Detroit Red Wings and two for the Chicago Blackhawks until his unpredictability compelled the Hawks to unload Young to the minors. He eventually reformed while playing minor league hockey and wound up in the majors again in 1974-75 with Phoenix of the WHA.

Zeidel

Few sports comebacks have ever been laced with the flair produced by defenseman Larry Zeidel in the summer of 1967. Zeidel was one of the few Jewish players in professional hockey, and in Yiddish there's a word for what he did — it's called chutzpah.

A rugged type, Zeidel had played briefly in the NHL for Detroit and Chicago before being demoted to the minors in 1954 where he played until 1967 when the National Hockey League expanded from six to 12 teams. In that year Zeidel, aged 39, compiled a flashy resume complete with a letter from a doctor stating he had the heart of a 22-year-old and sent the brochure to everybody important on each of the 12 NHL teams.

Every club but one said "thanks-but-no-thanks." The Philadelphia Flyers were willing to take a chance. Manager Bud Poile signed Zeidel and started him alongside Joe Watson. The Flyers began winning and Larry appeared to be playing better hockey than he had with the Cup champion Red Wings or the Blackhawks (1953-54).

On November 4, 1967 the Flyers were scheduled to meet tougher competition than they had met in their expansion division — the Montreal Canadiens. That afternoon Bernie Parent, then a young goalie, and Zeidel were in their hotel room where Parent had a bad case of the shakes. But Zeidel encouraged him to think "positive" and to have confidence in his ability.

Five hours later the game was over: Philadelphia 4, Montreal 1. Bernie Parent had thought "positive." A week later Philadelphia went to Boston and defeated the Bruins. A week after that Philadelphia defeated the Rangers. Zeidel started every game with Watson at his side.

The Flyers finished first, winning the Clarence Campbell Bowl, and Zeidel was among the best players on the club. Although the Flyers were eliminated from the playoffs, Zeidel appeared to be a fixture with the Flyers. But he had a dispute with Poile in the 1968-69 season. Poile wanted Zeidel to play in Quebec of the American League, but Zeidel refused. He retired from hockey in 1969 and went into the investment counseling business.

120 Significant Events in NHL History

1. Founding of NHL on November 22, 1917. Frank Calder was the first president.

2. Expansion to the U.S.: Boston is admitted to the league in 1924.

3. North America's biggest city, New York, gets NHL team (the Americans) in 1925.

4. Montreal becomes first NHL city with two teams. Maroons admitted in 1924.

5. Balance of power shifts from Canada to U.S. in 1926 with admission of three new U.S. teams — Rangers, Chicago and Detroit. Now there are six NHL clubs in the States and four in Canada.

6. First internationally known star on the scene, Howie Morenz, plays from 1923-24 until his death in 1937.

7. Death of Georges Vezina, greatest goalie of the 1920s and establishment of the Vezina Trophy. He died in 1926 and the first award of the trophy was in the 1926-27 season.

8. Flu epidemic in 1919 causes cancellation of playoffs after five games.

9. First NHL team to win the playoffs — Toronto Arenas, 1917.

10. Joe Malone's record-breaking scoring game. January 31, 1920; seven goals.

11. Schedule reaches 44 games per club (up from 22 in 1917), 1926-27.

12. Rangers manager Lester Patrick goes into goal against the Montreal Maroons in the Stanley Cup finals, April 7, 1928, at age 42.

13. Three playing zones and forward passing to center area come

into existence. Kicking the puck allowed (but not into goal) and tabulation of assists started, 1918-19.

14.   Goalies allowed to pass puck forward, 1920-21.

15.   Delayed penalty rule introduced. Never fewer than four players per team, 1925-26.

16.   The first 0-0 game, December 17, 1924 at Ottawa; Senators vs. Hamilton Tigers.

17.   Eddie Shore joins the Bruins; first superstar on an American team, 1926-27.

18.   Conn Smythe invited to organize the Rangers; he's fired before the season starts and eventually builds the Maple Leafs, 1926.

19.   Lester Patrick takes over the Rangers and fuses one of the NHL's greatest lines — Bill Cook, Bun Cook and Frank Boucher, 1926.

20.   New York becomes the first American city with two teams, Rangers and Americans, 1926.

21.   Stanley Cup playoffs in 1926 were the last between an NHL team and the West champions. Since the 1926-27 season the playoffs decide the Cup-winners.

22.   The last time an NHL team lost the Stanley Cup to a Western representative, 1925, Victoria Cougars beat Montreal Canadiens. All games were played in Victoria.

23.   First modern hockey arena in the United States opens; Madison Square Garden, 1925.

24.   Maple Leafs become contenders after Conn Smythe acquires ace defenseman King Clancy, 1930. The deal is only made possible after Smythe won a longshot bet at the race track.

25.   Eddie Shore nearly kills Ace Bailey in a vicious Boston-Toronto game, 1933. Bailey never plays hockey again.

26.   Howie Morenz united with Aurel Joliat and Johnny (Black Cat) Gagnon to form one of Montreal Canadiens greatest lines, 1930-31.

27.   Toronto's first Kid Line (Joe Primeau, Busher Jackson, Charlie Conacher), originally united on Christmas Day, 1929, broken up and reunited again.

28.   Conn Smythe launched Maple Leaf Gardens construction project, 1931. Work completed in record time.

29.   Chicago Stadium completed, 1929. Largest arena in the NHL.

30.   Great Depression takes its toll; NHL loses Ottawa, Philadelphia, Pittsburgh, St. Louis. By 1935 the league is down to eight teams.

One of hockey's greatest lines: (left to Right) Bun Cook, Frank Boucher and Bill Cook, shown here playing a benifit game a decade after each had retired.

31. First unofficial All-Star Game, played in honour of the injured Ace Bailey, 1933-34.

32. All-Star Team inception, 1930-31.

33. Frank Boucher wins so many Lady Byng Trophies, Lady Byng gives him the trophy and strikes a new one, 1936.

34. Charlie Gardiner, stricken with tonsilitis, plays entire playoffs in net for Chicago with illness and leads them to their first Stanley Cup, 1933. Gardiner died two months later in a Winnipeg hospital.

35. Foster Hewitt's first broadcast of a professional game, 1923.

36. Longest NHL game ever played — Detroit's Mud Bruneteau scored after 116:30 of overtime to defeat the Montreal Maroons, 1-0, March 24, 1936.

37. Maroons fold in 1938; no more two-team cities in Canada.

38. Americans beat Rangers in playoffs, 1938. Last New York-New York playoff series until Islanders arrive in 1972.

39. The death of Howie Morenz — the largest funeral for an NHL player, Nov. 2, 1937. That year's All-Star game is a Morenz benefit.

40. First Stanley Cup win for Detroit, 1936.

41. New York Rangers become first American NHL team to win Cup, 1928.

42. Opening of Boston Garden, 1928. Crowd breaks down doors to get in.

43. Frank Brimsek's rookie shutout string of 231 minutes, 54 seconds, 1938. Earns nickname Mr. Zero.

44. New York Americans change name to Brooklyn Americans but remain at Madison Square Garden, 1941.

45. Murray Murdoch sets first Iron Man record of 508 straight games, 1926-1938.

46. Chicago wins 1938 Stanley Cup with more American-born players than ever before.

47. Myles J. Lane becomes first All-America football star (at Dartmouth) to reach NHL (with the Bruins), 1929. He was the first American to play on a Stanley Cup winner.

48. First NHL players off to war, 1939-40.

49. Americans fold, 1942; leaves NHL with six teams and it stays that way until 1967.

50. Boston forms Kraut Line (Milt Schmidt, Woody Dumart, Bobby Bauer), 1936-37.

51. Greatest Stanley Cup comeback, 1942. Maple Leafs overcome 3-0 series deficit to down Red Wings in seven.

52. Legendary Maurice (Rocket) Richard plays first game for Canadiens, 1942.

53. During World War II, player shortages were so acute that teams did everything they could to fill rosters. Rangers coach Frank Boucher, who hadn't played since the 1937-38 season, came out of retirement for the 1943-44 campaign at age 42. He played 15 games and tallied four goals and 10 assists.

54. Overtime is abolished due to World War II schedules, November 21, 1942.

55. Frank (Ulcers) McCool records three straight shutouts in 1945 playoffs for Toronto to lead his team to Cup.

56. World War II ends, August, 1945; superstars return to NHL.

57. The immortal Gordie Howe plays his first game for the Red Wings, 1946.

58. Canadiens coach Dick Irvin creates Punch Line (Maurice Richard, Elmer Lach, Toe Blake), 1942-43.

59. Richard scores a record five goals in a Canadiens' 5-1 win over the Leafs, 1944.

60. Maple Leafs and Blackhawks complete biggest trade in NHL history, 1947. The five-for-two trade sends superstar Max Bentley to Toronto for a complete forward line and two defensemen.

61. Toronto becomes first team to win three straight Cups, 1947-49.

62. Toronto goalie Turk Broda wins the Vezina Trophy and Syl Apps scores his 200th career goal on the same night vs. Detroit in 1948.

63. Billy ("The Kid") Taylor and Don Gallinger banned for life for gambling, 1948.

64. Near-death of Gordie Howe in 1950 playoffs vs. Toronto. Howe missed check on Ted Kennedy and went crashing head first into boards.

65. Rangers play home games in Toronto in 1950; take Detroit to double overtime of seventh game in finals before losing.

66. Question raised about "Norris House League" after a major trade between the Norris-owned Red Wings and Norris-owned Blackhawks, 1946.

67. Worst hockey brawl, Canadiens vs. Rangers, Madison Square Garden, 1947. Montreal's Ken Reardon suffers a smashed mouth and exits for repairs. The Ranger bench rises as he leaves the ice, the Canadiens dash across the rink and every player is involved before the police riot squad is called in.

68. Mel (Sudden Death) Hill's exploits, 1939 playoffs. Hill, a 10-goal scorer in the regular season, comes to life at the right moments in Boston's semifinal series with the Rangers. Hill scores overtime game-winners in the first two games and scored the series winner in the third overtime of game seven.

69. Cleveland attempts to join NHL, 1951. Was rejected at eleventh hour.

70. Red Wings finish first for seven straight seasons, 1948-55.

71. Every game of the Leafs-Canadiens 1951 playoff series goes to overtime. Bill Barilko scores series winner for Toronto, then dies soon thereafter in a plane crash.

72. Joe Primeau becomes first coach to win the Memorial Cup, Allan Cup and Stanley Cup (1951).

73. Hap Day retires in 1950 after winning five Stanley Cups with Toronto, the only coach at that time with five championships.

74. Canadiens win five straight Stanley Cups, 1956-60.

75. After a protracted battle, Canadiens persuade Jean Beliveau to turn pro, 1951.

76. Henri ("Pocket Rocket") Richard signs with Canadiens in 1955, joining his brother Maurice.

77. Jacques Plante becomes first goalie to don a mask after taking a shot in the face at Madison Square Garden, 1959.

78. United States team wins Olympic hockey gold medal in 1960. Goalie Jack McCartan joins Rangers; first to draw major attention to American players in NHL.

79. Minnesota center Bill Masterton dies after collision during California Seals-North Stars game, January 15, 1968. Incident spurred rush by players to wear helmets, led by Stan Mikita.

80. NHL expands from six to 12 teams, 1967. Added are Philadelphia, Pittsburgh, Los Angeles, Minnesota, California and St. Louis.

81. Iron man goaltender Glenn Hall plays 552 consecutive games without a mask, 1955-64.

82. John Ferguson signs with Canadiens in 1963; advent of the enforcer in the NHL.

83. NHL Players' Association organized by Alan Eagleson, 1965.

84. Frank Calder dies in 1943 after 26 years as NHL president. Replaced by Red Dutton.

85. Dutton resigns in 1946. Succeeded by Clarence Campbell.

86. After 31 years as president, Campbell steps down in 1977. Replaced by John Ziegler.

87. NHL goes to war with upstart World Hockey Association, 1972. After active attempt to lure NHL superstars away, Bobby Hull jumps to new league.

88. NHL and WHA merge in 1979; Edmonton, Quebec, Hartford and Winnipeg increase number of NHL teams to 21.

89. First official All-Star Game played in Toronto, 1947.

90. Wayne Gretzky makes his NHL debut with Edmonton in 1979.

91. NHL Pension Society formed in 1948.

92. Gordie Howe skates on a line with his sons, Mark and Marty, with the WHA's Houston Aeros, 1973.

93. Islanders become first American team to win four straight Stanley Cups, 1980-83.

94. Center red line introduced, 1943. Idea hatched by Rangers coach Frank Boucher.

95. Philadelphia Flyers become first expansion team to win Cup, 1974.

96. Wayne Gretzky scores his 1,843rd point to break Gordie Howe's all-time scoring record, 1990.

97. NHL All-Stars play the Soviets in an eight-game series, 1972. Team Canada wins in the final 38 seconds of the last game.

98. Borje Salming leads the Swedish invasion of the NHL, 1973. Salming played with the Maple Leafs.

99. U.S. wins second Olympic gold medal, 1980. Win leads to massive influx of Americans into NHL.

100. Six Russians enter NHL, 1989. Vyacheslav Fetisov, Alexei Kasatonov, Sergei Makarov, Alexander Mogilny, Igor Larionov and Vladimir Krutov all suit up for the 1989-90 season, paving the way for numerous eastern European players to come to the NHL.

101. Canada Cup play launched by Alan Eagleson in 1976.

102. Longest playoff game of expansion era, April 18, 1987. The Islanders and Capitals played 68 minutes, 47 seconds of overtime in game seven of their first-round series before Pat Lafontaine ended it.

103. Red Berenson, first expansion superstar, scores six goals for St. Louis against Philadelphia, November 7, 1968.

104. Willie O'Ree becomes first Black hockey player in NHL with Boston, 1957.

105. Bill Stewart becomes first American-born coach to win Stanley Cup by leading Blackhawks to title, 1938.

106. Bob Johnson leads Penguins to 1991 Cup. Only other American-born coach to win championship.

107. Rocket Richard becomes first player to score 50 goals in 50 games, 1945.

108. Steve Smith shoots puck off Grant Fuhr and into Oiler net, giving Calgary a 4-3 series victory, 1986. Montreal goes on to win Cup, the only title from 1984-88 that doesn't belong to Edmonton.

109. Scotty Bowman's Canadiens win four straight Stanley Cups, 1976-79. Bowman then leaves the organization to take over in Buffalo.

110. Referee Andy van Hellemond works his 1,173rd NHL game — most ever by an NHL ref, 1991.

111. Bill Mosienko scores three goals in 21 seconds, 1951. Still stands as fastest hat trick in league history.

112. Bob Goodenow replaces Alan Eagleson as NHL Players' Association head, 1990.

113. Philadelphia goalie Ron Hextall scores a clean goal vs. Boston, December 8, 1987.

114. Whalers defenseman Mark Howe nearly killed crashing into net, 1980-81. Accident forces league to change net anchors from metal spikes to magnets.

115. Paul Coffey scores his 47th goal, breaking Bobby Orr's record for most goals by a defenseman in one season, 1986.

116. Quebec gets two Stastnys — Anton and Peter — compliments of Czechoslovakia, 1980.

117. Leafs center Darryl Sittler scores 10 points (six goals, four assists) in a game against the Bruins, February 7, 1976. Still an NHL record.

118. Edmonton defeats Islanders, four games to one, to take the Cup in 1984. First of five titles in seven seasons for the Oilers.

119. Brian Lawton chosen first overall in 1983 draft by Minnesota. First American player ever taken as top draft choice.

120. NHL players go on strike, delaying the start of the playoffs for 11 days, 1992. First strike in over 65 years and many of the key sticking points were left unresolved.

The Two Most Traded National Leaguers

When Brent Ashton started the 1991-92 seasons he thought he had found a permanent home in Winnipeg. At least he had hoped so.

Over a 13-year (now 14) career, Ashton had been traded six times for eleven players. He had played in seven different cities.

Ed Willes of the *Winnipeg Sun* recalled that during one memorable day of golf in Saskatoon, "Ashton started the round as a Vancouver Canuck, made the turn as a Winnipeg Jet and played the back nine as a Colorado Rockie."

In October 1991 Ashton had reason to believe that he would finish his career in Winnipeg. After all, he had been with the Jets longer than any other team — 218 games on October 10, 1991, with Quebec second at 172 games — and he had been getting good notices in Winnipeg.

But, lo and behold, he was dispatched to the Boston Bruins after only seven games as a Jet.

So, since 1979-80 when he launched his career with Vancouver, Ashton has played for the following clubs: Colorado, New Jersey, Minnesota, Quebec, Detroit, Winnipeg and Boston. Next stop? "At this stage in my career," says Ashton, "I'm happy to be playing anywhere!"

Tony McKegney's long journey through the NHL system began in 1978-79 when he was drafted by the Buffalo Sabres as the 32nd pick in the amateur draft. This would turn out to be Tony's longest stint with all of the seven different teams for which he would play. McKegney played five seasons for the Sabres before being shipped off on his first trade to Quebec. Tony would later return to Quebec in the 1989-90 season, after being dealt by the Red Wings.

Tony arrived in Quebec at the start of the 1983-84 season and played a year-and-half there before being sent to Minnesota during the 1984-85 campaign. This trade involved the two most traded players in the NHL, since the deal included Brent Ashton and Tony. Ashton's stay in Quebec wasn't long, nor was Tony's life in Minnesota. Early in the 1986-87 season, the North Stars sent Tony packing once again. This time he was headed off to the Big Apple, to be a part of the New York Rangers.

Tony's tenure in New York lasted only for the 1986-87 season, for he was immediately shipped off to St. Louis, where he would play two full seasons with the Blues. The start of the 1989-90 season brought about a trade to team number six, the Detroit Red Wings. Tony never seemed to fit in there, and 14 games into the season he was sent sailing back to his second NHL team, the Quebec Nordiques.

Tony would finish the 1989-90 season with the Nordiques and lasted more than half of the 1990-91 campaign with them. However, in January 1991, Tony was traded to his third Norris Division team, the Chicago Blackhawks, and he finished out the year with them.

In 1991-92 the 34-year-old McKegney laced up his skates in Europe.

THE MOST OFF-THE-WALL GOALIES

1. *Glenn Hall, Chicago Blackhawks, St. Louis Blues*
    Hall would vomit out of nervousness before every game. If the reverse peristalsis didn't come naturally, Hall would induce the vomiting himself.

2. *Jacques Plante, Montreal Canadiens, New York Rangers, St.Louis Blues, Toronto Maple Leafs, Boston Bruins, Edmonton Oilers*
    Plante's hobby was knitting "tuques" (wool hats) which he would wear throughout his junior and minor league career. When he tried to wear one in the NHL with the Canadiens, coach Toe Blake nixed the notion.

3. *Gilles Gratton, Toronto Toros, New York Rangers*
    "Grattoony," as he was known to teammates, implicitly believed that he had been reincarnated several times over and had once been a Spanish knight in the 14th century. He also is notorious as the only goalie in hockey history to have streaked (nude) across the ice. However, Gratton only did it at practice.

4. *Rogatien Vachon, Montreal Canadiens, Los Angeles Kings* During the 1970s, when players were wearing ridiculously long hair and sideburns, Vachon had one of the more arresting Fu Manchu moustaches and sideburns. "Zee sideburns," Vachon explained, "zey are good for zee balance."

5. *Ron Hextall, Quebec Nordiques*
    In the most annoying and fan-inciting manner, "Hexy" can be found slapping the base of his stick back and forth off both goal

posts and the crossbar before the start of each period and between each stoppage of play. Throw in the circular head movements that go along with his stick action and it makes for an unusual sight.

Ronnie has a passion for using his stick, and has been involved in three separate stick-swinging suspensions in his career. This is not your average goalie.

SCOTTY BOWMAN'S TWO FAVORITE GLENN HALL STORIES

1.   The Playoff Crisis

"I was coaching St.Louis in the Blues first season (1967-68), and even though we didn't finish first, we came on strong in the playoffs. Our first round opponent was Philadelphia, which did finish first in the division. During the regular season Philly had done well against us, but we beat them in seven games.

"Next we had Minnesota and they also gave us a hard time. Meantime, Glenn is playing great goal for us but, as always, was very nervous. Well, the series with the North Stars went to seven games and before the seventh game, Glenn was very down on himself. He kept asking me to keep an eye on him and I did.

"We had brought up Doug Harvey, the Hall of Fame defenseman, from our Kansas City farm team because they had been eliminated. In contrast to Hall, Harvey was the most relaxed guy in hockey. 'Doug,' I said, 'I want you to keep your eye on Glenn.' Harvey laughed. 'Don't worry, coach,' he replied. 'I'll keep both eyes on him.'

"So, now we're close to game time and Hall is a wreck. Meantime, I'm looking for Harvey who is supposed to be watching out for Hall, and where do I find Doug just before we're supposed to take the ice? He's calmly shaving. I couldn't believe it.

"Well, with Hall in such shape, I had my doubts about the game. But, it's a 1-1 tie after regulation and Glenn is just sensational. Then we go into overtime and still it's 1-1. Finally, in the second sudden death, Ron Schock scored for us and we went on to take the series. But without Hall we'd have been dead."

2. *The Painted Barn*

"Before Glenn came to St. Louis he had a long and distinguished career with the Chicago Blackhawks. Of course, he always worried and often told reporters that he hated goaltending. He once described it as 'Sixty minutes of hell.'

"One thing that he really didn't like was practices and another was training camp. When he played for Chicago he had to face Bobby Hull's blasts during the many scrimmages the team had and he could really blast the puck.

"Glenn invariably showed up late for training camp and the excuse he'd always give to reporters was that he hadn't finished painting his barn — 'and it is a real big one.' He always managed to leave the barn-painting for the days when training camp began.

"Because he was so good, Hall managed to get those extra days off to finish his barn-painting. Management figured they could spare it because Glenn was such a prize. Then, when he was taken in the expansion draft by St. Louis, Lynn Patrick, who was our general manager, and myself went to Stoney Plain (near Edmonton) to visit Hall at his farm.

"When we got to Stoney Plain, Glenn showed us around his property. Suddenly, I noticed that something was missing. 'Glenn,' I said, 'where's the barn?'

"He laughed. `There is no barn,' he said. 'Just lots and lots of acreage.'

"'But what about the barn you always said you were painting?' I asked, a bit naively.

"'I guess there never was one after all,'" said Glenn, and thus a major hockey hoax was revealed.

WORST CONDUCT BY HOCKEY FANS

1. *Garden Brawl I*
   In March, 1947, Montreal Canadiens defenseman Ken Reardon left the ice for repairs after his face had been bashed by Cal Gardner of the Rangers. As Reardon exited, a fan shouted, "You bum, you got what you deserved!" When Reardon turned in the fan's direction, players on the Rangers' bench rose to see what was happening. Across the ice, Montreal's bench noticed the hullabaloo and thought Reardon was being attacked by the Rangers. The entire Canadiens' squad raced across the ice, detonating one of the worst brawls in hockey history.

2. *Garden Brawl II*

   In November 1965, New York Rangers general manager Emile Francis took issue with a decision made by goal judge Arthur Reichert. Francis raced down the aisles to confront the official, but when Francis arrived at Reichert's spot, a couple of fans intercepted Francis and began berating him.

   Seeing that through the protective glass, several Rangers on the ice thought their boss was being assaulted by the fans. Led by Vic Hadfield, many of the Rangers, including Arnie Brown and Don Johns, vaulted the glass and engaged the fans in battle. The fur really flew for a while and, later, so did the lawsuits.

3. *Quebec Challenge*

   Late in the 1991-92 season, a Quebec fan bet with some friends that he would have the nerve to run out on the ice and challenge a member of the visiting Buffalo Sabres. The fan climbed over the boards and proceeded to challenge the Sabres while 14,000 Colisée fans looked on in amazement. Rob Ray and several Buffalo players punched him silly, including coach John Muckler.

The NHL record book has no listing for "Best Storming of the Crowd by Uniformed Players." If it did, Ken Hodge (8) and Derek Sanderson (hidden by Hodge) would certainly get mention for their 1970 foray into the stands at St. Louis Arena.

STRANGE HOCKEY TROPHIES

1. *Avco World Cup*
    The Stanley Cup is the most revered trophy in professional sports. When the World Hockey Association came on the scene in 1972, it felt obliged to strike a championship trophy of its own. Desperate for money, the WHA went the huckster route and found an outfit willing to pay big bucks to have its name on an annual trophy. Thus, the Avco Financial Services Company paid $500,000 cash to the league to have its name on the championship silverware. The Avco World Cup was awarded to WHA champions until the league merged with the NHL in 1979.

2. *Walker Cup*
    Jimmy (Beau James) Walker was the song-and-dance Democrat mayor of New York City during the Roarin' Twenties. Discredited by scandal in the early 1930s, Walker nevertheless was revered by New Yorkers and continued to be a part of the sporting scene. In the late 1930s, Beau James — a keen hockey fan — donated The Walker Cup to be awarded to the champion of the Eastern Hockey League. At the end of each season, Walker would make the presentation on Madison Square Garden ice. One year the Walker Cup was missing but, after a city-wide search, it was located in the window of a pawnshop down the street from the Garden.

3. *Greyhound Lines*
    Believe it or not, the renowned bus company, Greyhound Lines, awarded a trophy to the winner of the New York-New York series between the Rangers and the then-Americans. One photo exists of Americans defenseman Red Dutton receiving the trophy from a uniformed Greyhound driver.

1979 — THE BEST FIRST ROUND DRAFT OF THE 1970's

Selections	Claimed By
1. Rob Ramage	Colorado
2. Perry Turnbull	St. Louis
3. Mike Foligno	Red Wings
4. Mike Gartner	Capitals
5. Rick Vaive	Canucks
6. Craig Hartsburg	North Stars
7. Keith Brown	Blackhawks
8. Ray Bourque	Bruins
9. Laurie Boschman	Maple Leafs
10. Tom McCarthy	North Stars
11. Mike Ramsey	Sabres
12. Paul Reinhart	Flames
13. Doug Sulliman	Rangers
14. Brian Propp	Flyers
15. Brad McCrimmon	Bruins
16. Jay Wells	Kings
17. Duane Sutter	Islanders
18. Ray Allison	Whalers
19. Jimmy Mann	Jets
20. Michel Goulet	Nordiques
21. Kevin Lowe	Oilers

1984 — THE BEST FIRST-ROUND DRAFT OF THE 1980's

Selection	Claimed By
1. Mario Lemieux	Penguins
2. Kirk Muller	Devils
3. Ed Olczyk	Blackhawks
4. Al Iafrate	Maple Leafs
5. Petr Svoboda	Canadiens
6. Craig Redmond	Kings
7. Shawn Burr	Red Wings
8. Shayne Corson	Canadiens

9.	Doug Bodger	Penguins
10.	J.J. Daigneault	Canucks
11.	Sylvain Cote	Whalers
12.	Gary Roberts	Flames
13.	David Quinn	North Stars
14.	Terry Carkner	Rangers
15.	Trevor Stienburg	Nordiques
16.	Roger Belanger	Penguins
17.	Kevin Hatcher	Capitals
18.	Mikael Andersson	Sabres
19.	Dave Pasin	Bruins
20.	Duncan MacPherson	Islanders
21.	Selmar Odelein	Oilers

HOCKEY'S GREATEST TRAGEDIES

1. *Bill Barilko*
   The Toronto Maple Leafs defenseman scored the Stanley Cup-winning goal against Montreal Canadiens in Game Five of the 1951 finals. Bashin' Bill had become the most popular player in Canada. During the summer, Barilko and a friend, Dr. Henry Hudson, went on a fishing trip in Northern Ontario. Their plane crashed in dense woods. Innumerable searches failed to find the wreck until, finally, Barilko and Dr. Hudson were given up for lost. In 1962 the wreckage with the bodies was discovered.

2. *Howie Morenz*
   One of hockey's greatest stars in the late 1920s and early 1930s, Morenz had his best years with the Montreal Canadiens before being traded to the Chicago Blackhawks and then the New York Rangers. Just when it appeared he was washed up, Morenz returned to the Habs in 1936-37 where he regained his form. On January 28, 1937, Howie was bodychecked by a Chicago defenseman and suffered a broken leg. Morenz was expected to recuperate and, of course, play again. But inexplicably his condition took a turn for the worse and, on March 8, 1937, Morenz died in the hospital. A funeral service for Morenz was held at center ice of the Forum where thousands filed silently past his bier.

3. *Babe Siebert*

   An outstanding left wing, Siebert starred for the Montreal Maroons, New York Rangers and Boston Bruins from 1925 through 1939. After captaining the 1939 edition of the Canadiens, Babe was named coach of the team for the next season, but that was never to be. Tragically, Siebert drownedon August 25, 1939.

4. *Bill Masterton*

   A successful minor leaguer for several years in the early 1960s, Masterton got his first major break with the big-leaguers when he was signed by the Minnesota North Stars for the 1967-68 season. On January 13, 1968, Masterton was playing against the Oakland Seals at Metropolitan Sports Center in Bloomington when he tried to split the Seals defense of Larry Cahan and Ron Harris. They legally checked Masterton who fell to the ice. "He hit the ice so hard," said North Stars coach Wren Blair, "that I'm sure he was unconscious before he fell. I'd never seen anybody go down that way." Masterton never regained consciousness and died two days later. Beginning the next season, the NHL annually presented a Bill Masterton Trophy "for the player who best exemplifies the qualities of perseverance, sportsmanship and dedication to hockey."

5. *Georges Vezina*

   The outstanding goaltender in the early NHL years, Vezina was stricken with tuberculosis during the 1924-25 season, but he continued to play despite the ailment. That year he took the Montreal Canadiens to the Stanley Cup finals before they were beaten by Victoria. Still afflicted, Vezina returned for the 1925-26 campaign and was in net for the Habs on the night of November 28, 1925 at Mount Royal Arena. Overcome by a temperature of 105 degrees, Vezina struggled through the game until he no longer could see the puck. He finally collapsed in the crease. Georges Vezina had played his last game. He died on March 24, 1926, a week after the Canadiens had been eliminated from a playoff berth.

The Worst Number One Draft Picks from 1974 to the Present

1. Greg Joly, Washington, 1974.
2. Doug Wickenheiser, Montreal, 1980.
3. Brian Lawton, Minnesota, 1983.
4. Dale McCourt, Detroit, 1977.
5. Gord Kluzak, Boston, 1982. (Bad because of injury, not incompetence.)

The Conachers in Order of Their Ability

In terms of the 20th century, the Conacher family of Toronto is considered the royal sports clan of Canada. Lionel, the oldest of the brothers, was voted Canada's athlete of the half-century (1900-1950). Several Conachers played in the NHL including Lionel's son, Brian. Herewith, the Conachers in order of their ability:

1. *Lionel*
   Not only was he Athlete of the Half-Century, he was an All-Star NHL defenseman and a three-sport star. In Canadian football he became known as The Big Train. As a defenseman, he played for the Pittsburgh Pirates, New York Americans, Montreal Maroons and Chicago Blackhawks.

2. *Charlie*
   Acclaimed as the hard-shooting member of Toronto's Kid Line with Joe Primeau and Busher Jackson, Charlie surpassed 200 goals when that was a huge accomplishment. He won the Art Ross Trophy in 1934 and 1935 and was a three-time First Team All-Star at right wing. He also played for the Detroit Red Wings and New York Americans.

3. *Roy*
   The youngest of the three to make it to the NHL, Roy was a crack left wing with the Boston Bruins and later the Detroit Red Wings and Chicago Blackhawks. He, too, surpassed 200 goals and was scoring champion in 1949 and First Team All-Star.

4. *Brian*

   Lionel's son, Brian arrived with the Toronto Maple Leafs in 1966-67 after starring in the minors. The Leafs won the Stanley Cup in 1967 and Brian was a prominent figure in the victory. "I was strictly a journeyman," he said, "but I happened to be in the right place at the right time." He later moved to the World Hockey Association and then became a hockey executive.

5. *Pete*

   Charlie's son (actually he was Charles, Jr. but preferred to be called Pete) couldn't handle the pressure after being rushed to the NHL with the Chicago Blackhawks in 1951-52. He was traded to the New York Rangers in November 1954 and finished his career in minor league obscurity.

   P.S.   A nephew of the Conacher brothers, Murray Henderson, played eight NHL seasons on the Boston Bruins defense during the late 1940s. Pat Conacher, who most recently played for the New Jersey Devils, is not related to the clan.

THE MOST BEAUTIFUL BRETT HULL GOAL

Playing against the New York Islanders on December 21, 1991 at St. Louis Arena, the Blues were at the very top of their game. But nobody could surpass Hull. He took the puck in his own end and went through the opposition to score. The move was so awesome that the Arena press box at first was quiet until Bob Ramsey observed, "Hull is god!"

THE MOST BEAUTIFUL STANLEY CUP COMEBACK GOAL

In Game One of the 1992 Stanley Cup finals between the Pittsburgh Penguins and Chicago Blackhawks at Pittsburgh's Civic Arena, the visitors jumped into 3-0 and 4-1 leads. The home club kept chipping away and reduced the deficit to one goal in the third period. Chicago's defense held tight until there was but minutes remaining. At that point Jaromir Jagr of the Penguins captured the puck and proceeded to bob and weave through three Blackhawks defenders in extremely close quarters. Jagr worked his way into scoring position and then released a backhander that beat goalie Ed Belfour. With the score tied, Mario Lemieux then scored the game-winner. The Penguins then went on to win the next three straight games and their second consecutive Stanley Cup.

The Two Best Demolished Old Rinks

1. *Madison Square Garden*
   Located at Eighth Avenue between 49th and 50th Streets near Times Square, "The Old Garden" was home to the New York Rangers and New York Americans from its opening in 1925 to its razing in 1968. It was a three-tiered rink featuring a mezzanine and upper balcony.

2. *Olympia Stadium*
   Longtime home of the Red Wings, the Olympia was located at Grand River and McGraw. It was slightly smaller than Madison Square Garden and also featured balconies. Players remember it fondly for the curious geography of the rink. There was an eggshaped design that frequently caused strange rebounds off the boards.

The Most Incredible Family of Hockey Broadcasters

1. *Marv Albert*
   He has been the Rangers' play-by-play broadcaster since 1965, although he also handles network baseball, basketball and football.

2. *Al Albert*
   Marv's next younger brother, Al handled the Islanders' play-by-play on radio in their first season, 1972-73, and later did the New Jersey Devils telecasts. He has since moved on to basketball.

3. *Steve Albert*
   Youngest of the Albert trio, Steve broke in doing Cleveland

Crusaders' games in the World Hockey Association and later was a SportsChannel play-by-play man for Devils' telecasts.

4. *Kenny Albert*
Marv's oldest son, the New York University graduate, began as a statistician for his father and last season became play-by-play man for the Baltimore Skipjacks of the American League. He launched his NHL career in October 1992 as Washington Capitals' play-by-play telecaster.

THE ALL-TIME BEST HOCKEY BROADCASTERS

1. *Foster Hewitt*
He not only was the original — handling Toronto Maple Leaf games — he was inimitable. Foster was the first to shout, "He Shoots! He Scores!" and became the most imitated man in sportscasting.

2. *Doug Smith*
This will surprise a lot of people because he wasn't around all that long. But Smith called the Montreal Canadiens' games in the late 1940s and was special enough to compete with Hewitt although, to Doug's credit, he never attempted to ape Foster.

3. *Bill Hewitt*
In the period during which he followed his father, Bill carried on the Hewitt tradition to a T and was wonderful to listen to just as Foster was.

4. *Danny Gallivan*
Many critics consider Gentleman Dan the dean of hockey broadcasters (after Hewitt, of course) and much can be said for that. Gallivan's articulation was impeccable and his selection of expressions had a special quality to it that endeared him to millions of Canadiens' fans.

5. *Dan Kelly*
The success of the St. Louis Blues in their first years of operation during the late 1960s was due as much to Kelly's stirring broadcasts as to the team itself.

ALL-TIME ARENAS LIST

Loudest:

1. *Chicago Stadium*
   For starters, you have the most rabid fans in the league; rooters who begin cheering with the start of the "Star Spangled Banner." Then there's the arena architecture; the two balconies overhang the ice giving an extremely "close" feel in which the noise level is accentuated. And almost every game is sold out.

2. *Boston Garden*
   Many of Chicago Stadium's qualities listed above hold for Boston except that "The Gahden" is somewhat smaller and therefore less noisy. The Bruins draw a blue-collar crowd that just loves to yell.

3. *Madison Square Garden*
   Manhattan fans are the most obscene, animalistic, ignorant and otherwise boorish, but they are loud, and when their New York Rangers are winning the decibel count often drowns out the referee's whistle.

Quietest:

1. *Northlands Coliseum*
   Edmonton fans were spoiled by Wayne Gretzky & Co. and too many Stanley Cups. The spectators seem more like readers in a library than rooters.

2. *Hartford Civic Center*
   Even when the Whalers were winners, it was difficult to get emotion in the crowd. Some observers believe it is symptomatic of the Insurance City.

3. *Maple Leaf Gardens*
   Part of the problem in Toronto has been the team. The Leafs have been so bad for so long, fans have forgotten how to root. This could change with a winner.

Top Five Defunct Jerseys

1. *New York Americans*
   The perfect marriage between the American flag and a hockey sweater. All the variations over the years were more interesting than the blah Rangers' uniform.

2. *Toronto St. Patricks*
   Simplicity in its finest sense. White base, accompanied by a green clover.

3. *Quebec Bulldogs*
   Effective use of yellow, blue and white. It may sound boring but photos of Phantom Joe Malone prove its appeal.

4. *Montreal Maroons*
   An eye-catching maroon tone with a varsity style "M" in the middle. It's a classy sweater that accentuated the club's professionalism.

5. *Colorado Rockies*
   The Rockies only significant impact in the NHL came in the form of their uniforms. White, blue, yellow and red fashioned with a mountain peak. It provided a unique design for a franchise about which there was little to boast

Pass Me the Smelling Salts

One of the NHL's most unusual pre-game rituals involved Montreal Canadiens forward Mike McPhee, goalie Patrick Roy, the Canadiens trainer and smelling salts.

Before each match, the trainer handed McPhee a smelling salt. After a quick sniff, McPhee tossed the salt to Roy. When the catch was made, McPhee acknowledged his goaltender with a complimentary, "Great save, Pat!"

Best Hair Piece Wearers in the NHL

1. *Guy Lafleur*
   The Flower began losing his mane with the Montreal Canadiens and dropped more hair when he made his comeback with the Rangers. After moving back to Quebec City, Guy found a hairstylist who has provided him with a mane that now is magnificent.

2. *Bobby Hull*
   As a youngster with the Chicago Blackhawks, the Golden Jet had a renowned blond mop. By the time Hull moved to the World Hockey Association, it had developed a bald spot. Bobby finally found a hairpiece that has restored him to leonine glory.

Two Incredible Single Game Playoff Comebacks

1. *Penguins, 1992*
   Trailing the Chicago Blackhawks 3-0 and 4-1 in Game One of the finals, the Pittsburghers rallied to tie the count late in the third period and won the game on Mario Lemieux's powerplay goal in the final minute.

2. *Blues, 1986*
   Huge underdogs, the St. Louis sextet trailed the Calgary Flames three games to two going into Game Six of the Campbell Conference championship at St. Louis Arena. The Blues trailed 4-1 and 5-2 in the third period before rallying to tie the count whereupon Doug Wickenheiser won the game for St. Louis in overtime.

The Two Most Unusual Ways of Calling a Goal

1. *The Eichler Automatic Goal Judge*
   During the mid-1940s, Rangers' broadcasts were sponsored by a local brewery which produced Eichler Beer. The beer's theme

was "It's The Tops," alluding to the rich head of foam on the top. For commercial purposes, Eichler borrowed the Cole Porter tune "You're The Tops" to laud its foam. With this in mind, brewery engineers constructed a device which would play the first notes of "You're The Tops" when the Rangers scored a goal. Play-by-play man Bert Lee would activate the device and tell fans "And here's the Eichler Automatic Goal Judge," whereupon it would beep out the first three bars of "You're The Tops."

2. *Mike Lange-isms*
Pittsburgh Penguins' broadcaster Mike Lange is the most original of the contemporary hockey announcers. Instead of bellowing the traditional, "He shoots! He scores!", Lange is known to blare forth with, "Rip my shirt off and scratch my back with a hacksaw." Or, "Elvis has left the building", among other gems.

THE WORST REASON TO BE SENT TO THE MINORS

When Conn Smythe operated the Toronto Maple Leafs in the late 1940s, he ran a tight ship. One of Smythe's regulations pertained to matrimony. He believed it was ill-advised for his players to get married in mid-season. But two players, Johnny (Goose) McCormack and William (Wild Bill) Ezinicki disobeyed the boss. Result: both were sent to the Pittsburgh Hornets, a minor league affiliate, for punishment.

SPEED KILLS

It is often said that skating is the most important asset in becoming a successful hockey player, yet three of the best skaters ever to set foot on NHL rinks failed to make an impression.

1. *Leo Gravelle*
Nicknamed "Gravelle The Gazelle," Leo played for the Montreal Canadiens and Detroit Red Wings during the 1946-1951 period. While his skating drew oohs and ahhhs, his production left much to be desired.

2. *Norm Dussault*
   A Canadiens forward during the Gravelle Era, Stormin' Norman was a pint-sized version of Gravelle. Lots of style; little
   substance.

3. *Gene Carr*
   He broke in with the St. Louis Blues in 1971 and later played for
   the New York Rangers and Los Angeles Kings. If ever there was
   a case of a player going nowhere fast — in a hurry, Carr was it!

THE THREE MOST MIS-SPELLED NAMES IN NHL HISTORY

1. *Terry Sawchuk*
   Ninnies and non-historians usually spell it Sawchuck, which is
   very, very wrong.

2. *Jim Thomson*
   The Toronto Maple Leafs crack defenseman of the late 1940s and
   early 1950s suffers the same fate as baseball hero Bobby Thomson.
   The unknowing invariably spell it Thompson. Nay, nay, NAY.

3. *Walt Tkaczuk*
   Once a highly rated New York Rangers center, Walter's problem was that he pronounced it "Ka-chook" and that got just
   about everybody crazy. "As a result," says his former agent,
   Larry Rauch, "almost everyone spelled Walter's name wrong."

ALL-TIME BLOOD FEUDS

1. *Ken Reardon — Cal Gardner*
   In a March 1947 New York Rangers-Montreal Canadiens game
   at Madison Square Garden, defenseman Reardon's face was
   badly mashed in a collision at center ice. For some time, Reardon
   was unaware of the assailant, but when Rangers defenseman
   Hal Laycoe was traded from New York to Montreal and became
   a Canadiens teammate of Reardon, he tipped him off that Cal

Who owned the most mispronounced name in hockey history? Walt Tkaczuk, shown here in full stride. New Yorkers said "Tay-chuk".

Gardner had done the damage. By this time Gardner had been dealt to the Toronto Maple Leafs but Reardon had not forgotten. He and Gardner wound up in one of the NHL's most vicious stick and fist fights. Later Reardon told a reporter from *Sport* magazine that he was going to "get" Gardner. NHL president Clarence Campbell was so incensed he forced Reardon to post a cash bond insuring that he would not injure Gardner for the rest of his career. Reardon complied. Long after both had retired they refused to acknowledge one another at old-timers games.

2. *Maurice Richard — Ted Lindsay*
   The Rocket of the Montreal Canadiens and Terrible Ted of the Detroit Red Wings were bitter rivals during the late 1940s and early 1950s. "Lindsay always played dirty with me," said Richard. Once, Lindsay harassed Richard without receiving a penalty in a Saturday night game. The Rocket was so furious that on Sunday he collared the referee Hugh MacLean in a New York hotel and wound up suspended for it. The bitterness never abated. "I saw the two of them play in a no-checking old-timers game," said Associated Press reporter Ben Olan. "Everybody else was enjoying himself, but The Rocket and Lindsay wound

up having a fight. And they were as intense as they had been in their prime."

3. *Don Cherry — Harry Sinden*
It was the Bruins general manager, Sinden, who gave Grapes his first break as an NHL coach. Cherry, in turn, converted the Bruins into an exciting, lunchpail team in the late 1970s. While he was at it, Cherry became a character in his own right and often got more publicity than his players. Sinden believed that Grapes was getting too big for his britches and the inevitable collision took place. Cherry was fired and never forgave Sinden for the rupture. They have continued sparring ever since with no losers. Cherry became a wealthy, popular television personality and restaurateur while Sinden is still running the Bruins.

WORST DECISION BY A REFEREE AND LINESMAN IN NHL HISTORY

On May 8, 1988 the New Jersey Devils and Boston Bruins were to play Game Four of their Wales Conference championship series at Byrne Meadowlands Arena. Game Three had ended with a major eruption when Devils coach Jim Schoenfeld angrily confronted referee Don Koharski in the hallway following the game.

Although Schoenfeld had been temporarily suspended by the league, the Devils went to court and won a decision allowing Schoenfeld to coach in Game Four which just happened to be on Mother's Day. The referee for that game was to be Dave Newell along with linesmen Gord Broseker and Ray Scampinello.

Upon learning that Schoenfeld would coach in the game, Newell, Broseker and Scampinello refused to take the ice and, in effect, went on strike.

The league was determined to have the game played. When NHL supervisor John McCauley realized that the officiating trio meant business, he recruited three amateur officials — Paul McInnis, Vin Godleski and Jim Sullivan. With McInnis doing the refereeing, the local zebras did a splendid job under the circumstances; better, no doubt, than Newell, Broseker and Scampinello would have done.

WORST UNIFORMS IN HOCKEY HISTORY

1. *Philadelphia Flyers*
    In the early 1980s a couple of hockey suppliers designed a uniform that replaced the traditional stockings and short pants uniform with long pants that extended from the waist to the skates. The Flyers were the first to experiment with them and were so thoroughly criticized they eventually returned to the normal uniform.

2. *Hartford Whalers*
    They tried the Flyers' experiment, with the same results.

3. *Brooklyn Americans*
    In their last season (1941-42) in the NHL, the New York Americans made a desperate attempt at luring fans to Madison Square Garden by changing the club's name from New York to Brooklyn Americans. The team continued playing in New York but moved its practice rink to the Brooklyn Ice Palace. Likewise, the Amerks abandoned their colorful star-spangled uniforms and switched to an ugly, bland jersey which simply had the word BROOKLYN across the front. It impressed no one and the club folded the following spring.

THE MOST RELEVANT HOCKEY PEOPLE WHO'S LAST NAME BEGINS WITH "N"

1. *Lou Nanne*
    A former player, coach, general manager and executive with the Minnesota North Stars.

2. *Vaclav Nedomansky*
    One of the first super-Czech stars to play pro in North America. He broke in with the WHA's Toronto Toros in 1974 and later played in the NHL.

3. *Jim Neilson*
    A husky, half-Cree native, The Chief played more than a decade on defense in the NHL, starting in 1962.

4. *Eric Nesterenko*
Originally billed as the English version of Jean Beliveau, Nester was less than that as a Toronto Maple Leaf (1951-56) and later with the Chicago Blackhawks. He later became a ski instructor.

5. *Bob Nevin*
Right wing on a strong line with Red Kelly at center and Frank Mahovlich on the left, Nevin played for three straight Toronto Maple Leaf Stanley Cup-winners from 1962-64.

6. *Frank Nighbor*
The Hall of Famer who finished his career with the Toronto Maple Leafs in 1930, won the Hart Trophy in 1924 and the Lady Byng Trophy in 1925 and 1926.

7. *Reg Noble*
Mister Versatility played defense, left wing and center starting with the Montreal Canadiens in 1917 and finishing with the Detroit Falcons in 1932.

8. *Bruce Norris*
He was the last member of the Norris Family to own the Detroit Red Wings.

9. *James Norris*
Father of Bruce and the original owner of the Red Wings.

10. *James D. Norris*
Older brother of Bruce and son of James. He became Red Wings owner and also was a partner, with Arthur Wirtz, in the Chicago Blackhawks.

11. *Marguerite Norris*
She was the first female president of a hockey team, taking over the Red Wings upon the death of her father, James Norris, in 1952.

12. *William Northey*
He supervised construction of the Montreal Forum.

Most Underrated Player by Decade

1990s — Craig MacTavish

He's the last of the helmetless Edmonton Oilers and a tenacious forward who laboured too long in the shadows of Mark Messier, Wayne Gretzky et. al.

1980s — John Tonelli

No question, the New York Islanders would not have won four straight Stanley Cups (1980-83) without the hard-driving left wing. He personally saved them on April 13, 1982 by almost single-handedly beating the Pittsburgh Penguins who had pushed the Isles to the brink of elimination.

1970s — Bob Gainey

Guy Lafleur, Jacques Lemaire, Steve Shutt, Ken Dryden and other Montreal Canadiens were getting all the credit for the four straight (1976-79) Stanley Cup wins but Gainey was doing all the work.

1960s — Dick Duff

The smallish left wing launched the Toronto Maple Leafs on their three-consecutive Stanley Cup streak in 1962 at Chicago Stadium with the Cup-clinching goal at 14:14 of the third period of Game Six. He was traded to the Montreal Canadiens in 1965 and, guess what, they began winning Cups again.

1950s — Don Marshall

When the Montreal Canadiens were winning an unprecedented five Stanley Cups in a row (1956-60), they did it, in part, with strength down the middle. The top centers were Jean Beliveau and Henri Richard. But right behind them was the utilitarian Marshall who could do everything — take a regular turn, work the powerplay or kill penalties, the latter of which he did better than most.

1940s — Nick Metz

The Toronto Maple Leafs executed the most incredible comeback in the history of the Stanley Cup finals. They were down 3-0 in games to the Detroit Red Wings in the 1942 playoffs. With incredible aplomb, the Leafs rebounded to win four in a row. No other team has ever accomplished that feat in the finals. Metz —

his brother, Don, also was a hero — galvanized the Leafs and remained an unsung hero on later Toronto Cup teams in 1945, 1947 and 1948. On top of that he was one of the first premier penalty killers in the NHL.

1930s — Bill Cowley

When one thinks of Boston Bruins heroes, the names of Eddie Shore, Milt Schmidt and Frankie Brimsek often come to mind. But Bill Cowley was one of the most gifted centermen stickhandlers who maintained a high standard of excellence through his retirement in 1947. He was especially adroit in the 1939 Boston Stanley Cup win.

1920s — Murray Murdoch

The NHL's first iron man, Murdoch played in 508 consecutive games, starting with the 1926-27 season. He completed 11 NHL seasons without missing a game up to his retirement after the 1936-37 season. Murdoch was a hard-nosed left winger who always got the job done without any fuss or fanfare.

THE NHL PRESIDENTS IN ORDER OF THEIR ACCOMPLISHMENTS

1. *Frank Calder*

   He was the first, getting the job in 1917, and automatically gets first prize for staying in power for 26 years. Calder's throne was vacated only because of his death on February 4, 1943. During that time he presided over expansion to the United States and contraction to six teams at the time of his passing. He was an excellent tool of his bosses, the owners.

2. *Red Dutton*

   Upon Calder's passing, Dutton agreed to assume the presidency on an interim basis. Give him credit; he got out while the getting out was good, lasting until 1946 when he joined his family's construction business.

3. *John Ziegler*

   In 1977, Ziegler — the NHL's first American-born president — took over from overrated Clarence Campbell. At the time the

NHL was being bled white in a war with the World Hockey Association. Ziegler helped effect a merger with the WHA and later helped turn the NHL into a money-making operation. He maintained labour peace into the 1990s but was hurt by a strike in 1992. Often aloof and officious, Ziegler suffered terribly with the media and finally resigned in 1992.

4. *Clarence Campbell*
Essentially a puppet for the owners, Campbell saw the NHL through an early 1950s crisis when one or two teams nearly folded. He opposed expansion but caved in when pressured. During his reign, the NHL was a low-budget antediluvian operation that did not change until the advent of John Ziegler. A mini-scandal late in his career somewhat tarnished Campbell's reputation, but he did manage to get a conference named after him.

GREAT HOCKEY QUOTES

1. "DEFEAT DOES NOT REST LIGHTLY ON OUR SHOULDERS."
— Message enscribed by Toronto Maple Leafs manager Conn Smythe on the club's dressing room wall.

2. "TO YOU WITH FAILING ARMS, WE THROW THE TORCH, BE YOURS TO HOLD IT HIGH" — From the poem "Flanders Fields" by John McCrae, on the Canadiens' dressing room wall.

3. "IF YOU CAN'T BEAT 'EM IN THE ALLEY, YOU CAN'T BEAT 'EM ON THE ICE." — Conn Smythe commenting on winning hockey.

4. "SPREAD OUT!" — Advice shouted from NHL benches to lone defenseman confronted by a two-on-one break.

5. "THE TROUBLE WITH THIS TEAM IS THAT EVERYONE THINKS WE HAVE A GEORGE ON THE ROSTER AND THEY WANT TO 'LET GEORGE DO IT.' UNFORTUNATELY, WE DON'T HAVE A GEORGE ON OUR TEAM." — Coach Toe Blake complaining about his Montreal Canadiens in 1956.

6. "THEY'RE GUTLESS, CHICKEN . . . AND PRINT IT!"
— Coach Phil Watson ridiculing his New York Rangers in 1958.

7. "THE WORLD HOCKEY ASSOCIATION WILL NEVER GET OFF THE GROUND." — NHL President Clarence Campbell talking to reporters at the Plaza Hotel in New York in 1971. A year later the WHA not only got off the ground but cost the NHL millions of dollars.

8. "HOCKEY IS A GAME OF MISTAKES." — New York Rangers manager Lester Patrick in 1939.

9. "HOCKEY IS A SLIPPERY GAME . . . IT'S PLAYED ON ICE!" — New York Rangers general manager Emile Francis explaining a loss to reporters in 1969.

10. "VERY LITTLE MATTERS, AND NOTHING MATTERS VERY MUCH." — *New York Times* hockey writer Joseph Nichols, explaining why he doesn't get excited about wins or losses while covering the game.

Toe Blake holds the unofficial NHL record for "Hardest Door-Slamming Coach." So, how come he was calm enough to win the Lady Byng trophy in 1946 as a Montreal Canadiens right winger?

All-Time Lopsided Trades

1. *Bruins Get Rick Middleton*
    New York Rangers general manager John Ferguson listened too closely to his center Phil Esposito who was unhappy in New York. The homesick Espo wanted company from his former team, the Boston Bruins. He prevailed on Ferguson to obtain his erstwhile linemate Ken Hodge from Beantown. Fergie relented and sent young, gifted Rick Middleton in exchange on May 26, 1976. Hodge was an abject bust on Broadway. Middleton became a sensation with the Bruins, reaching the 103 point mark in 1980-81. By that time, Hodge had long since retired.

2. *Bruins Get Phil Esposito, Ken Hodge and Fred Stanfield*
    The date was May 15, 1967. Chicago Blackhawks general manager Tommy Ivan believed that Esposito would not be a superstar nor that Ken Hodge would be a better-than-average scorer. Thus, Espo, Hodge and the fourth-string Stanfield went to Beantown. Ivan had hoped that defenseman Gilles Marotte would be a super defenseman and that Pit Martin would emerge as a better-than-average center. Goalie Jack Norris, the third man in the deal, was a question mark. Esposito blossomed into a Hall of Famer. Hodge was a very good scorer and Stanfield one of the most underrated forwards of the 1970s. Espo was the catalyst for the Bruins' two Stanley Cup triumphs in 1970 and 1972. Marotte was a disaster on defense and Martin only an average forward. Norris was completely nowhere in goal.

3. *Maple Leafs Get Max Bentley*
    In the fall of 1947 Toronto Maple Leafs general manager Conn Smythe was still glowing over his spring Stanley Cup win. However, he also felt he needed more strength down the center to complement his aces Ted Kennedy and Syl Apps. His eye was on Chicago Blackhawks pivot Max Bentley. The Hawks had been going nowhere fast and needed lots of bodies. Smythe dealt them an entire forward line — Gus Bodnar, Bud Poile and Gaye Stewart, dubbed The Flying Forts because they all hailed from Fort William, Ontario — and a pair of defensemen, Bob Goldham and Ernie Dickens. Critics thought that the Blackhawks won on sheer numbers but it was not so because Bentley was one of hockey's best centers. He helped the Leafs to Stanley Cups in 1948, 1949 and 1951. Despite their five acquisitions, the Blackhawks didn't even

make the playoffs until six years after the trade by which time only Bodnar remained.

4. *Glenn Hall to Chicago*
    Detroit Red Wings general manager Jack (Jolly Jawn) Adams was given to impetuous moves and the one which cost him the most dearly was made in July 1957. Adams erroneously blamed young goalie Glenn Hall for a playoff defeat and resented left wing Ted Lindsay for attempting to launch a players' union. In retribution he dealt both to the Chicago Blackhawks. In return Adams received forwards Johnny Wilson, Forbes Kennedy, and Bill Preston as well as goalie Hank Bassen. Wilson was an adequate player while the others were fringe at best. Hall went on to become one of hockey's most accomplished goaltenders while Lindsay remained an inspirational player.

5. *Rod Langway to Washington*
    No trade did more to turn around a franchise than the one engineered by Washington Capitals general manager David Poile on September 9, 1982. He knew that Rod Langway was unhappy in Montreal and obtained the defenseman along with another young backliner named Brian Engblom as well as forwards Craig Loughlin and Doug Jarvis. Poile gave up two once-promising top draft picks, defenseman Rick Green and forward Ryan Walter. While Green and Walter played decently enough for the Habs, Langway became a giant with the Caps, winning a pair of Norris Trophies and leading the team to the playoffs for the first time in franchise history. Langway went on to become captain while Jarvis flowered into one of the finest defensive forwards. Engblom became an anchor of the defense and Loughlin was a useful utility forward.

TWENTY BEST CURRENT PLAYERS LISTS

Goalies
1. Patrick Roy; 2. Kirk McLean; 3. Tom Barrasso; 4. Ed Belfour; 5. John Vanbiesbrouck; 6. Bob Essensa; 7. Mike Richter; 8. Bill Ranford; 9. Curtis Joseph; 10. Andy Moog; 11. Chris Terreri; 12. Tim Cheveldae; 13. Jon Casey; 14. Don Beaupre; 15. Grant Fuhr;

16. Kelly Hrudey; 17. Ron Hextall; 18. Jeff Hackett; 19. Rick Tabaracci; 20. Mike Vernon.

Left Wingers

1. Kevin Stevens; 2. Gary Roberts; 3. Luc Robitaille,; 4. Vincent Damphousse; 5. Esa Tikkanen; 6. Pavel Bure; 7. Kirk Muller; 8. Adam Graves; 9. Dave Andreychuk; 10. Brendan Shanahan; 11. Shayne Corson; 12. Brian Bellows; 13. Bob Probert; 14. Craig Simpson; 15. Kelly Miller; 16. Sergio Momesso; 17. Tony Granato; 18. Wendel Clark; 19. Steve Thomas; 20. Michel Goulet.

Right Wingers

1. Brett Hull; 2. Mark Recchi; 3. Trevor Linden; 4. Rick Tocchet; 5. Cam Neely; 6. Jaromir Jagr; 7. Mike Modano; 8. Joe Murphy; 9. Steve Larmer; 10. Alexander Mogilny; 11. Claude Lemieux; 12. Paul Ysebaert; 13. Mats Sundin; 14. Russ Courtnall; 15. Joe Mullen; 16. Owen Nolan; 17. John MacLean; 18. Pat Verbeek; 19. Stephane Richer; 20. Kevin Dineen.

Centres

1. Mario Lemieux; 2. Jeremy Roenick; 3. Mark Messier; 4. Wayne Gretzky; 5. Pat LaFontaine; 6. Steve Yzerman; 7. Pierre Turgeon; 8. Joe Sakic; 9. Sergei Fedorov; 10. Adam Oates; 11. Doug Gilmour; 12. Rod Brind'Amour; 13. Craig Janney; 14. Dale Hawerchuk; 15. Dimitri Khristich; 16. Theo Fleury; 17. Bernie Nicholls; 18. Michal Pivonka; 19. Jimmy Carson; 20. Benoit Hogue.

Defensive Defensemen

1. Ulf Samuelsson; 2. Ray Bourque; 3. Scott Stevens; 4. Steve Smith; 5. Mark Tinordi; 6. Brad McCrimmon; 7. Dave Manson; 8. Alexei Kasatonov; 9. Craig Muni; 10. Jamie Macoun; 11. Jim Johnson; 12. Rod Langway; 13. Vladimir Kostantinov; 14. Mark Hardy; 15. Frank Musil; 16. Kjell Samuelsson; 17. Jeff Beukeboom; 18. Mike Ramsey; 19. Garth Butcher; 20. Joe Reekie.

Offensive Defensemen

1. Brian Leetch; 2. Phil Housley; 3. Paul Coffey; 4. Chris Chelios; 5. Ray Bourque; 6. Larry Murphy; 7. Kevin Hatcher; 8. James Patrick; 9. Al MacInnis; 10. Al Iafrate; 11. Steve Duchesne; 12. Scott Stevens; 13. Fred Olausson; 14. Gary Suter; 15. Dave Ellett; 16. Jeff Brown; 17. Nicklas Lidstrom; 18. Zarley Zalapski; 19. Dave Manson; 20. Glen Wesley.

THE TWO MOST DIFFICULT NAMES
CONFOUNDING PUBLICISTS

1. *Steve Wojciechowski*
   He played for the Detroit Red Wings in the mid-1940s and so baffled hockey writers and public relations people that the Wings had his name changed to Wochy for ease-of-spelling purposes.

2. *Enio Sclisizzi*
   This was another tongue-twister with Detroit and then Chicago in the late 1940s. His full name was Enio James Sclisizzi. Again the Detroit wordsmiths went to work and altered it to Jim Enio.

BEST TOURISTY PUTDOWN OF A PLAYER BY A
COLUMNIST

During the 1991-92 season, *Manchester* (Connecticut) *Journal-Inquirer* columnist Randy Smith was covering the Hartford Whalers. Smith took a dim view of the fact that high-paid Whalers forward John Cullen seemed to be dropping to the ice as often as he was skating. Smith suggested that the Hartford Chamber of Commerce send brochures to travel agencies with the inscription, "COME TO HARTFORD AND SEE CULLEN FALLS."

DEREK SANDERSON'S FOUR MAJOR
ACCOMPLISHMENTS AS A PLAYER

1. He was the most underrated of the Big, Bad Bruins who won Stanley Cups in 1970 and 1972.

2. He was the first NHL player to pose semi-nude in *Life* magazine.

3. He was the first NHL player to co-author two autobiographies — *I've Got To Be Me* (Dodd Mead) and *The Derek Sanderson Nobody Knows* (Follet) within three years.

4. He was the first NHL defector into the World Hockey Association to purchase a Rolls-Royce.

John Ziegler's Eight Biggest Mistakes as NHL President

1. He disappeared during the 1988 Devils-Bruins' playoff crisis and to this day nobody knows where he was at the time.

2. His media relations were somewhere below minus-the-radical 50.

3. He appeared to spend more time in Europe than he did in North America.

4. He rarely was seen at NHL games.

5. He closed the league's New York public relations department leaving the NHL as the only one of the four major sports without a publicity presence in the world's media capital.

6. He fought — rather than listened to — his friends who became critics.

7. He couldn't be found in the spring of 1992 when Mario Lemieux was chopped down by Adam Graves and a presidential decision was being demanded by the public.

8. He ridiculed his employers — the 24 NHL governors — by saying that the league needed a union-management partnership. "We need someone to protect the owners from themselves!"

Two Best Comebacks From Seemingly Insurmountable Injuries

1. *Mark Fitzpatrick*
   The New York Islanders goalie became afflicted with a rare and incurable disease. It had been predicted that he would never play hockey again. Nevertheless, Fitzpatrick — using medicine to control the ailment — returned for the 1991-92 season and played commendably for the Isles. He also won for the league's Bill Masterton Trophy.

2. *Doug Wickenheiser*
   The Wick's career supposedly was ended after he was struck on the knee by an oncoming car after slipping off the back of a pickup truck while trying to climb in during a team outing in Eureka, Missouri. The damage to Wickenheiser's knee was so extensive it was believed that even reconstructive surgery would not help. But the forward worked diligently in rehabilitation and eventually made it back to the bigs.

FOUR REASON'S WHY ERIC LINDROS WON'T BE AS GOOD AS THE MONEY HE'S PAID

1. His mother, Bonnie, will interfere too often in team affairs and get management crazy.

2. Every opponent and his Uncle Dudley will want to take a crack at Lindros — and will.

3. Lindros has a short fuse. He'll be fighting more than necessary and inevitably will break a finger on some foe's helmet. After the third time, he won't be able to shoot as well.

4. Nobody can be as good as Lindros' mountain of press clippings.

TWO GUYS WHO GOT IT BACKWARDS

1. *Pat Doyle*
   He was the public address announcer at Madison Square Garden who was delivering lineups during a New York Rangers-Toronto Maple Leafs encounter. At the time the Leafs had a top defenseman named Kent Douglas. Doyle called him "Douglas Kent."

2. *Gus Kyle*
   A former NHL defenseman, Kyle became a St. Louis Blues broadcaster during the days when Bob Plager was on defense. On one occasion the fiery Plager took exception to a referee's call, blew his stack and began hurling black, rubber missiles from the bench. Kyle observed, "Bob Plager just threw a puck of pails onto the ice."

THE THREE MOST OVER-PAID NHL PLAYERS

1. *Doug Wilson, $1 Million*
   Not bad for a washed-up defenseman whose best hockey was long ago left in Chicago.

2. *John Cullen, $1.2 Million*
   Perhaps sometime in the near future, this amiable chap will earn his keep. But who deserves more than a mill for 26 goals and 51 assists for 77 points in 1991-92? And he was minus-28, worst on the Whalers!

3. *Denis Savard, $1.25 Million*
   The Canadiens brought him in for marketing purposes. They wanted a name French-Canadian and they got him, but at what price? Surely, 28 goals, 42 assists and 70 points in 77 games aren't worth half that figure.

THE 100 BEST PLAYERS OF ALL TIME

1. Gordie Howe; 2. Mario Lemieux; 3. Wayne Gretzky; 4. Eddie Shore; 5. Red Kelly; 6. Frank Boucher; 7. Maurice Richard; 8. Howie Morenz; 9. Jean Beliveau; 10. Doug Harvey; 11. Glenn Hall; 12. Syl Apps; 13. Denis Potvin; 14. Bobby Orr; 15; Bobby Hull; 16. Bryan Trottier; 17. Bill Cook; 18. Max Bentley; 19. Georges Vezina; 20. King Clancy; 21. Nels Stewart; 22. Mike Bossy; 23. Lester Patrick; 24. Marcel Pronovost; 25. Paul Coffey; 26. Toe Blake; 27. Bernie Geoffrion; 28. Henri Richard; 29. Dickie Moore; 30. Joe Primeau; 31. Frank Mahovlich; 32. Milt Schmidt; 33. Ted Kennedy; 34. Mark Messier; 35. Charlie Conacher; 36. Bobby Clarke; 37. Jacques Plante; 38. Aurel Joliat; 39. Marcel Dionne; 40. Terry Sawchuk; 41. Ted Lindsay; 42. Phil Esposito; 43. Doug Bentley; 44. Frank Frederickson; 45. Bill Durnan; 46. Brad Park; 47. Turk Broda; 48. Bryan Hextall; 49. Tim Horton; 50. Art Coulter; 51. Guy Lafleur; 52. Bill Cowley; 53. Ching Johnson; 54. Sweeney Schriner; 55. Stan Mikita; 56. Bullet Joe Simpson; 57. Yvan Cournoyer; 58. Dale Hawerchuk; 59. Sid Abel; 60. Johnny Bower; 61. Ken Dryden; 62. Dit Clapper; 63. Bill Mosienko; 64. Hobey Baker; 65. Black Jack Stewart; 66. Cooney Weiland; 67. Dave Keon; 68. Babe Pratt; 69. Charlie Gardiner; 70. Syd Howe; 71. Dick Irvin; 72. Cyclone Taylor; 73. Frank Brimsek; 74. Duke Keats; 75. Billy Smith; 76. Peter Stastny; 77. Babe Dye; 78. Ray Bourque; 79.

Red Dutton; 80. Chuck Rayner; 81. Bob Gainey; 82. Georges Vezina; 83. Bill Quackenbush; 84. Bernie Parent; 85. Roger Crozier; 86. Carl Brewer; 87. Guy Lapointe; 88. Kevin Lowe; 89. Grant Fuhr; 90. Mark Howe; 91. Rod Langway; 92. Gerry Cheevers; 93. Hap Day; 94. Andy Bathgate; 95. Denis Savard; 96. Allan Stanley; 97. Gump Worsley; 98. Brett Hull; 99. Alex Delvecchio; 100. Larry Robinson.

Whenever anyone talks of the greatest Players of all-time, Boston's revolutionary defenseman Bobby Orr is always mentioned.

THE BEST ALL-BLACK LINE

It remains hard to believe that an all-black forward line not only thrived but starred for several years during the 1940s in two of the fastest hockey circuits in North America: the Provincial Hockey League (Quebec) and the Quebec Senior Hockey League.

The black unit was comprised of brothers Herbie and Ossie Carnegie from Toronto, playing center and right wing, and Manny McIntyre of Fredericton, New Brunswick, on left wing. "They would have been good enough to star in the NHL today," claims Larry Zeidel, a former NHL defenseman, who played against them in the Quebec League. "But in those days the NHL was a six-team league paying awfully low salaries. Ossie and Herbie were making terrific money in the Quebec League and had side jobs which gave them even more security. There was no reason to try for the NHL."

At one time or another the Toronto Maple Leafs and New York Rangers expressed interest in Herbie Carnegie, the best of the three, but hockey did not have an owner with the courage and foresight of Branch Rickey who brought Jackie Robinson into major league baseball. So, the Carnegies and McIntyre did their thing in the cities through Quebec and when the Quebec Senior League went international during the 1946-47 season, the line terrorized teams in New York and Boston with their dipsy-doodle brand of passing and skating.

Those who remember the Carnegies in their halcyon years believe that they reached their peak during the 1945-46 season, when they were playing for Sherbrooke Rand in the Provincial League which provided the bankroll as well as jobs for the team. The league had five other cities: Lachine (Montreal), Victoriaville, Drummondville, St. Hyacinthe and Cornwall, Ontario (about 60 miles from Montreal). Travelling time never exceeded a three-hour bus drive, unless a blizzard intervened. Teams played in compact arenas — average capacity 3,500-of pre-war vintage, frequently without heating. Spectators generally wore their overcoats throughout the game and visited the refreshment areas for warmth between periods. Few records remain from the long-defunct league, but one man vividly recalls the exploits of the only all-black line in hockey. He is Richard Wilson and in 1945 he was a young sportswriter for the *Sherbrooke Daily Record*. The following is Wilson's recollection of the Carnegie Brothers and Manny McIntyre. "Believe me, black was beautiful long before it became a civil rights slogan. That all-black hockey line on the white ice was one of the prettiest sights anybody could ever hope to see in sports. Sure, they played in a small league, in small buildings, but there was nothing small about the excitement they generated.

"Herbie Carnegie, who centered the line, was as good as any hockey player around. He had all the standard moves plus a couple of his own specialties. He excelled in all departments — stick-handling, passing, playmaking, shooting, forechecking, backchecking, penalty-killing, and speed.

"On the right wing, Ossie didn't have the speed, flash or dash of Herbie, but he always did a workmanlike job with one hundred percent effort. He was stronger, physically, than the other two, possessed a blazing shot, and played excellent positional hockey. Ossie was particularly effective in the corners where he could hold his own with any defenseman in the league.

"Manny worked left wing with the same discipline that Ossie showed on the right. He was a fine positional player, good in the corners, and willing to mix it with any challenger. A big man, McIntyre could hold his own when the going got rough; which sure was often in the Provincial League. If Manny had a weakness it was to pass instead of shoot. He was a good passer and playmaker and had twice as many assists as goals. His talents complimented the Carnegie brothers perfectly.

"As an all-black forward line they were an instant gate attraction. Transcending that novelty, however, their individual and combined hockey talents never failed to excite the fans. Ovations from partisan home crowds around the circuit were not uncommon.

"The best way to describe the line is to say that they always were in tune. You might call it three-part harmony. They knew each other's moves and anticipated each other so well it was impossible for a checking unit to hold them off the scoreboard very long."

BEST MAGIC TONIC

Leone's Magic Elixir, 1950-51
The brew was concocted by Broadway restauranteur Gene Leone for the oft-losing New York Rangers. Their record was well below .500 by early December 1951, when Leone perfected his formula and poured it into a large black bottle about three times the size of a normal whiskey bottle. With appropriate fanfare, "Leone's Magic Elixir" was carried into the Rangers dressing room where players such as Don "Bones" Raleigh, Pentti Lund, and Zellio Toppazzini quaffed the brew. After drinking the mixture, the Rangers began to win and win and win. By early January they had lost only two of their eleven games. Opponents became frightened. The Toronto Maple Leafs attempted to have Customs men seize the tonic when it arrived at the Toronto airport. *New York World Telegram* hockey writer Jim Burchard was placed in charge of the brew on road trips. Once, when the Rangers lost to Detroit, Burchard explained, "The Leone brew wasn't on deck. Without it, the Rangers were under a psychological handicap." After the loss, an SOS was dispatched to Leone, who quickly prepared more of the liquid and the Rangers whipped Toronto the next night. Eventually, the psychological value of the elixir ran its course and the Rangers faded to fifth place, out of the playoffs.

BEST NICKNAME

Georges Vezina, Montreal Canadiens
Because he hailed from Chicoutimi, Quebec, and was cool as a cucumber when he played, Vezina was called "the Chicoutimi Cucumber." Vezina was so accomplished that the goaltender's prize, the Vezina Trophy, was named after him.

BEST BALD-HEADED REFEREE

George "Gertie" Gravel
During the late Forties, the National Hockey League boasted an official whose pate was shinier than an eight ball. Gravel, a French-Canadian, was not only extremely efficient but also equally amusing. Once, in Chicago Stadium, a fan fired a dead fish at Gravel. He

picked it up by the tail in very delicate fashion, held it away from his body with one hand, held his other hand to his nose, skated over to the boards and deposited the fish near a woman spectator. With that she shouted: "Gravel, I hate you!"

Seemingly penitent, Gravel looked at the woman with soulful eyes and shook his head sadly: "Lady," he replied, "tonight I even hate myself."

Another time Ted Lindsay of the Detroit Red Wings executed a swan dive, hoping that he would inspire Gravel to penalize a Ranger player. While Lindsay remained horizontal on the ice, feigning injury, Gravel skated up to the Detroit player and calmly observed: "Ted, the ice is too hard for diving; and you can't swim in it either."

It's hard to believe that a referee could officiate in the NHL for more than a decade with only one good eye, but Bill Chatwick (center) did just that. He's flanked by ex-zebras Frank Udvari (left) and Cooper Smeaton.

BEST LITTLE GUY

Aurel Joliat
There isn't much room for 135-pounders in the National Hockey League, but Aurel Joliat was one who prospered in the league back in the Twenties. Joliat succeeded with shifty stickhandling and quick moves. The Montreal Canadiens traded the popular Newsy Lalonde to get Joliat, and the little guy responded by joining with Howie Morenz and Johnny "Black Cat" Gagnon to form a high-scoring line.

Joliat was no flash in the pan. He played in Montreal for 16 years, and was good enough to win the Hart Trophy as most valuable player in 1934, and be elected to the Hall of Fame.

Today people talk about the increasing number of big men coming into the sport, and how the players are better athletes than in the past.

After leaving hockey, Joliat ran a grocery store, worked for the Canadian National Railway and the Quebec Liquor Commission. He lived in Ottawa and said he had "absolutely no interest" in hockey, but did not hold the same aversion to skating.

"A couple years ago," he recalled, "on a mild night about two in the morning, I skated the whole canal in Ottawa, which is over five miles in length. I'm expecting a call from the pros any day now."

BEST MANAGER

Frank Selke, Sr., Montreal Canadiens
When Selke, who had been assistant manager in Toronto, moved to Montreal in 1946, the Canadiens organization was in a state of disintegration. Selke organized a farm system which, to this day, is the best in hockey. By 1950 the system had produced such stars as Jean Beliveau, Dickie Moore, Doug Harvey, Tom Johnson, Bernie Geoffrion, Phil Goyette, Claude Provost, and Andre Provonost. Selke's machine was so awesome that he was persuaded to stock the weak NHL clubs with "average" Montreal players. Thus, Selke dispatched Ed Litzenberger to the floundering Chicago Blackhawks and Litzenberger soon became a star. When Selke retired in 1960, the Canadiens had won six Stanley Cup championships. What's more, he left the nucleus of a team that would win seven more.

Best Long-Distance Challenge

Dawson City, Klondike, Canada, 1905
Shortly after the Klondike gold rush had subsided, a number of rich miners from Dawson City in Northwest Canada decided that it was time the Klondike was represented in Stanley Cup competition. The miners assembled a team and challenged the powerful Ottawa (Ontario) Silver Seven team to a championship series in the Canadian Capital. The Klondike team traveled more than 4,000 miles by the most primitive means of transportation, including dog sled. Undaunted, the boys from the Northwest invaded Ottawa in January 1905 and, to the surprise of many, almost made a contest of the first match. They ultimately were defeated, 9-2, but it was enough to kindle hopes that the second match would be even closer, if not a triumph for the Dawson City Skaters. But the bubble burst in the second game. The final score was Ottawa 23, Dawson City 2. Frank McGee, the one-eyed Ottawa Star, scored 14 goals, a Stanley Cup record.

Worst Attempted Fix

"Did you ever hear how I tried to fix it for Convey to be a star?" Francis Michael (King) Clancy would tell enchanted listeners, recalling the time Clancy arranged to keep a former Maple Leafs player in the league by making him look good. The player was Eddie (Cowboy) Convey, a less-than-adequate left wing for the New York Americans in 1933 whose play constantly invited demotion to the minor leagues.

One night the Americans visited Toronto and Convey's old pals heard through the grapevine that their former teammate needed a big game to survive in the NHL. Clancy's concern prompted him to conspire with Charlie Conacher, the large, blunt right winger, and Lorne Chabot, the tall, dour goalkeeper. "Look," Clancy told them before the game, "if we get a few goals up, let's make it easy for Convey. Let's help him score a couple."

The Leafs romped ahead 4-0 in the first period, far enough for Convey to get a chance — with Clancy's skilled collusion. Convey got off the Americans bench in the second period and, for a hilarious few minutes, it was as though the stage had been manipulated. He was on against Conacher on the Toronto forward line, Clancy on the Toronto defense, Chabot in the Toronto goal. "Now," Clancy muttered to Conacher as Convey skated down the wing. Conacher obligingly fell down to let him through. Convey walked in on Chabot, who didn't move. He had a clear shot at the open side of the net — and drove the puck wide.

"One more chance!' Clancy called to Conacher and Chabot and, soon, the cowboy again came riding down the wing. Conacher faked a bodycheck, and missed, Clancy stumbled and fell down. Convey swept in on the stationary Chabot, who left one side of the goal unprotected. Convey boomed a drive, high into the seats.

"One more time!" Clancy commanded, and Convey got it, the next time he appeared on the ice. "Let him through!" Clancy shouted at Conacher, who let Convey sail past. He escaped Clancy's bogus check.

As he told the tale, Clancey would ape Convey's lumbering motions. "He flew by me, really danglin', and went cruisin' in on Chabot, who was ready to step aside. He took careful aim and shot. Chabot fell to leave the whole goal open and Whap! Convey hit him right in the Adam's apple with the puck! Down he went, chokin' and gaggin'!"

Conacher skated back to help Clancy assist the distressed Chabot. "Any more of this," Chabot said, when he could speak, "and Convey'll kill me!"

"I guess we better knock off fakin' for him," Clancy suggested.

"Right," Conacher said, not concealing his disgust. "Forget Convey!"

WORST PLAYING CONDITIONS DURING A GAME

During game three of the 1975 Stanley Cup finals, the fans in Buffalo's War Memorial Auditorium got a glimpse of what hockey must look like in Foggy Old London. The Philadelphia Flyers and Buffalo Sabres were forced to decide the Stanley cup championship in a peasoup-like atmosphere. The 70 °F heat combined with the ice and the players' movements to produce a screen of fog which made seeing the puck almost impossible — particularly for the goalies, Bernie Parent of the Flyers and Roger Crozier of the Sabres.

"I couldn't see any shots from center ice," said Parent. "I'm sure it was the same for Crozier."

The game had to be delayed 11 times because of the thickness of the fog. During each unscheduled intermission, several arena attendants were called out onto the ice to fan the fog with a sheet, at least temporarily.

When that failed, the players came out and skated around the fog-congested area to keep it from building up. The only players who weren't annoyed at the delays were the fourth stringers on both teams who received more ice time than they had in weeks.

WORST GAME BY A TEAM

New York Rangers, January 23, 1944
Playing at Olympia Stadium, Detroit, the Rangers lost to the Red Wings by the record-breaking score of 15-0. Although the Rangers had been a first place team as recently as 1942, their roster was decimated by World War II. Coached by Frank Boucher, the New York sextet employed a mediocre goaltender named Ken "Tubby" McAuley who was more a victim of his inefficient defense than his own goaltending shortcomings.

WORST COACH

Emil Everson, Chicago Blackhawks, 1931-32
The flamboyant owner of the Blackhawks, Major Frederic McLaughlin, was determined to hire as many American-born hockey people as possible; thus, Iverson qualified for the Chicago coaching job on the basis of one factor — he was an American. As for his other credentials, they included a stint as a figure skater and experience as a physical culturist. He had never before coached a hockey club. Fortunately, Iverson did not coach very long. However, McLaughlin kept Iverson on the payroll with the title of physical director of the Blackhawks.

WORST STUNT

During the 1950-51 NHL season, a hypnotist made his one and only appearance in a rink to participate in a team's fortunes. The Rangers, who had encountered a series of misfortunes, decided to employ a Dr. David Tracy, who claimed to be a psychologist and hypnotist. Dr. Tracy had contacted Rangers publicist Herb Goren. He said he had been watching the Rangers lose and was convinced he could help the New York club start winning again if he had permission to do a little with the players.

Goren approached his boss, Rangers manager Frank Boucher, and urged Boucher to let Dr. Tracy do his thing, no matter how bizarre it might have appeared. "Dammit all, Frank," said Goren, "it can't do any harm. Let's try it. For sure we'll get good publicity out of the stunt.'

Boucher agreed on the theory that anything so unique might loosen up his anxiety ridden team. Dr. Tracy was given the green light and reported to Madison Square Garden a few hours before the game. Here are Boucher's recollections of what transpired:

"He came into our dressing room an hour or so before a game with Boston. He was a burly, jowly man with sleek black hair, beautifully tailored clothes, and he had a peculiar eye. There was a white dot in it that made him look very odd indeed.

"He was particularly attentive to Tony Leswick at the beginning, staring into his eyes and talking quietly while Pentti Lund, Alex Kaleta, and Buddy O'Connor sat in front of their neighboring lockers, listening closely. He spoke to all the players, but when it came to Nick Mickoski's turn, Nick fled from the room. He was afraid the guy was going to hypnotize him. Then the doctor spoke to the room at large, stressing positive attitudes, talking quietly, and purposefully. He needed to; we'd lost twelve in a row.

"We played a great game, too. The Garden was jammed, after the excellent coverage accorded the Tracy experiment, and we went into that final minute deadlocked with the Bruins, 3-3. But then Bill Quackenbush, a Boston defenseman, broke the spell with a long shot that hopped crazily over Charlie Rayner's stick, and we lost, 4-3.

"Tracy told me that two things worked against him. First, he shouldn't have undertaken the experiment at the moment of our thirteenth game without victory and second, he should have spent more time with Charlie Rayner. That doctor said that Charlie wasn't relaxed.

"Frankly, I thought the players had responded pretty well to the psyche-prober, but when he couldn't get us past our thirteenth hurdle I concluded the experiment. Tracy couldn't put the puck in the net or keep it out any better than I could."

MOST UNUSUAL PRESS AGENT

Hockey has had its share of classic press agents and one of the best was Jack Filman, a native of Hamilton, Ontario, who became the Rangers publicist in their first season. Filman was given to poetic license and, like many press agents, was wont to stretch the facts. In a publicity release he once explained the origin of hockey, claiming that North American Indians invented the game and called it "hogee." Pressed about the veracity of the term, Filman insisted that it was the correct word. "'Hogee' in English," said Filman, "means 'it hurts.'"

Jack always started the day with a mouthful (not a drink) of gin while making up the Rangers program. It's been said that one of the funniest sights was watching Filman in consultation with the printer's son when he came to collect the copy for the program. Since the printer's son was deaf and dumb and Filman had a mouthful of gin, nobody spoke. "With signs and gestures," said a Ranger official, "the two of them laboured over the layout, shaking their heads vigorously and pointing furiously with never a sound emanating from either one of them."

This is a rare one. This man was director of the famed Captain Video television show, and also was the New York Rangers' practice goalie. The late Arnee Knocks was also an accomplished jazz organist.

BEST GOAL

Maurice "Rocket""Richard, Montreal Canadiens vs. Boston Bruins, April 8, 1952.

No athlete has ever absorbed the physical abuse in a single game suffered by Richard, nor ever rebounded to score a more spectacular goal than Richard did in the final game of the Boston-Montreal Stanley Cup semifinals of April 1952. With the score tied, 1-1, in the second period, Richard was smashed to the ice from behind by Boston's Leo Labine. The unconscious Richard was carried off the ice, his body so limp some feared he was dead. He recovered in the dressing room and insisted upon returning to the bench, although coach Dick Irvin, fearful for Richard's health, had no intentions of using him again in the game. "After receiving his stitches, Richard was in a partial coma,' said a Montreal newsman. "His head was fuzzed with pain, his eyesight impaired, with dull noises ringing in his ears."

Nevertheless, in the third period Richard insisted upon playing. Late in the period, with the score still tied, he leaped off the bench, took a pass from teammate Butch Bouchard, and circled the Boston defense before shoving the puck past goalie Jim Henry. The goal was so dramatic that Richard's hard-nosed teammate Elmer Lach, who was sitting on the bench at the time of the score, leaned forward onto the sideboards and fainted. Thanks to Richard, the Canadiens won the game.

The pain had not subsided when Richard fell onto the bench in Montreal's dressing room. His father, Onesime Richard, walked in and put his right arm around the Rocket's shoulders and hugged his son. Hockey's greatest scorer no longer could control himself and he simply broke down and cried.

BEST SINGLE PERFORMANCE BY A FORWARD

Bill Mosienko, Chicago Blackhawks, March 23, 1952

The Blackhawks leading scorer had been the lone bright spot for the Chicago six in an otherwise unmemorable season. It was the final game of the 1951-52 schedule and pitted Mosienko's club against another nonplayoff — bound team, the Rangers.

In a span of 21 seconds during the third period, the Chicago right winger propelled his way into the National Hockey League record book by blasting three goals past substitute Ranger goaltender Lorne Anderson. The performance eclipsed the record of 1:04 by Carl Liscombe of the Detroit Red Wings in 1938. By himself, Mosienko also broke the team record for the fastest three markers by three seconds, originally set by Hooley Smith, Babe Siebert and Dave Trottier of the Montreal Maroons in 1932.

"The funny thing was," said Mosienko, in the dressing room after finishing the season with 31 goals, "that just a few seconds later, I was alone again. I faked Anderson out of position, and had an open goal to hit — and shot wide."

Best Single Performance by a Defenseman

Ian Turnbull, Toronto Maple Leafs, February 2, 1977
This steady but low-scoring blue liner treated Maple Leaf Gardens fans to a record night as he blasted an incredible five goals into the Detroit Red Wings' net. After a scoreless first period, Turnbull rocketed two shots past Detroit goalie Ed Giacomin in the second session and recorded three more goals in the third stanza at the expense of substitute goalie Jim Rutherford.

With his unexpected outburst (he hadn't scored a goal in the previous thirty games), Turnbull became the first defenseman in NHL annals to score five times in a game, breaking the previous standard of four, shared by five other players — none of whom played after 1937-38. The old record had stood for 47 years.

Best Fight

Montreal Canadiens vs. New York Rangers, Madison Square Garden, New York, March 16, 1947
The *New York Sun* called it "an almost endless fight." The *New York Times* classified it as "the grandest mass riot in the local history of the NHL." There was bad blood between the Canadiens and Rangers that season, and almost all of it was spilled during the contest.

Kenny Reardon, the rambunctious Montreal defenseman, had one thing in mind as he stickhandled across the Rangers' blue line with 32 seconds left in the game, which the Canadiens were leading, 4-3 — freeze the puck.

As Reardon carried the puck into the New Yorkers' zone, he

committed a cardinal hockey sin — he fixed his eyes on the black rubber disk and forgot to look where he was going. The next thing he knew, Bryan Hextall's hip loomed menacingly in front of him.

Reardon bounced off Hextall like a pinball right into Cal Gardner's waiting stick which obligingly bludgeoned Reardon across the mouth. "My upper lip," Ken said, "felt as if it had been sawed off my face."

The injured Canadien passed the Rangers' bench on the way to the medical room and overheard Ranger Phil Watson complain that Kenny's mangled lip was not nearly punishment enough for him. Reardon then bolted for Watson, but was intercepted by a policeman. Then up popped a balding fan brandishing a fist. "Reardon," he shouted, "I've been waiting a long time for you to get it. You louse."

"That did it," Reardon says. "I swung my stick at him — then a cop grabbed me from behind and I fell." The disturbance aroused the Rangers who rose from their seats out of natural curiosity. From a distant vantage point of the Montreal bench across the ice it appeared that the entire New York team was preparing to pounce upon Reardon.

"Get the hell over there," implored Montreal coach Dick Irvin to his players, while standing on his bench. And the Flying Frenchmen poured over the boards. Montreal captain Butch Bouchard, who led the stampede, clouted the bald-headed spectator with his stick while goalie Bill Durnan and Maurice Richard sought other prospective victims. Within seconds the Rangers wiped out Montreal's beachhead, forcing the invaders to regroup at center ice, where four main events were in progress: 1) Maurice Richard vs. Bill Juzda; 2) Bill Moe vs. Bill Durnan; 3) Hal Laycoe vs. Leo Lamoureux; 4) Butch Bouchard vs. Bryan Hextall. The Marquis of Queensbury would have sanctioned the Moe-Durnan and Laycoe-Lamoreux bouts, but the others were strictly back-alley affairs.

Moe, who had been ordered not to play because of a shoulder injury, floored the heavily padded Durnan with a roundhouse right. Laycoe and Lamoreux flailed away at each other in a fierce toe-to-toe encounter that ended only because the belligerents were too tired to throw another punch.

Meanwhile, Richard broke his stick over Judza's head, snapping the shaft in two. Judza arose slowly and tackled Richard, bringing him down violently. Then Bouchard ripped Hextall's stick away from him and flattened him with a punch. Having dispensed with Durnan, Moe cracked a stick over Bouchard's head and Butch didn't even seem to notice that he had been hit. Judza then excused himself from Richard, picked up a stray stick and poleaxed Buddy O'Connor, breaking his jaw.

The only players to escape unblemished were the normally violent Phil Watson of the Rangers and George Allen of Montreal. Watson says it wasn't an accident. "I grabbed ahold of Allen," Watson explains, "and said, 'Look George, what's the sense of getting all tangled up? Whaddya say we stand on the side and watch this one?' He said okay, so we did. It was the best fight we ever saw."

BEST PUTDOWN

Hap Day worked for the Toronto Maple Leafs from the day the franchise was born, first as player, later as coach. During his coaching reign, he led the club to five Stanley Cups in eight years. One would think that Day would be rewarded for his accomplishments. However, manager Conn Smythe did not agree. Instead of rewarding Day, Smythe fired him so he could give the job to his son, Stafford Smythe.

The story goes that Day later went into the tool handle business (what else?). A while later, he sent an axe handle to Conn Smythe, his former boss who, not knowing what to do with an axe handle, called Day to find out where he could find the blade. "Between my shoulder blades," Day replied, "where you put it!"

BEST FIBBING PEPTALK

Toronto Maple Leafs manager Conn Smythe, prior to the 1949 Stanley Cup playoff round
Smythe's Leafs had won the Stanley Cup two years in a row (1947 and 1948), but the manager believed that his men were becoming complacent with success. Smythe called his players together before the series began and delivered a lecture that was worthy of Knute Rockne or Vince Lombardi. One of the more impressionable of the Leafs at the time was center Cal Gardner.

"Connie," Gardner recalled, "gave us a pep talk about the brave Canadian soldiers who were with him at Vimy Ridge in World War I, and he mentioned my father as being one of the greatest. I guess it worked on me because I played my best game of the season that night and we won. After the game, the thought struck me about the great 'con job' Smythe had done on me. My father wasn't even in the army because of a gimpy leg."

THE TWO CLASSIC CHOKES

"C-H-O-K-E" is the Dirtiest Word in Hockey

Up until the Seventies, it was heretical even to allude to a hockey team or player as a choker. But the New York Rangers made a "choke" a respectable term simply by choking so many times during the coaching reign of Emile Francis that not only was it possible to discuss the art of getting the apple with a Ranger, but New York newspaper headline writers freely referred to the Rangers as the "Broadway Chokers."

The modern Rangers, however, were amateurs when it came to choking compared with past NHL clubs, including an earlier New York team. Compared with the Detroit Red Wings of 1941-42 and the 1958-59 Rangers, more recent chokers just couldn't hold an apple to them.

By far the classics of them all were the Red Wings of 1941-42 because they had the Stanley Cup in their grasp, having won the first three games of the final series against the Toronto Maple Leafs. But then they did something no other NHL team had ever done in Stanley Cup competition — they lost the next four Cup final games in a row and thereby blew a world championship.

The 1958-59 Ranger club had a comfortable nine point lead in the race for a playoff berth in the last month of the season. Then they fell apart like a house of cards and finally lost their playoff berth on the final night of the season under extraordinary circumstances. It was by far the worst choke during a regular season.

What made these two teams so unique, so collapsible? Consider the circumstances that follow:

Detroit Red Wings 1941-42

World War II was in full fire when manager Conn Smythe of the Maple Leafs and Jack Adams of the Red Wings were putting the finishing touches on what they hoped would be major hockey powers.

Smythe had made much more progress than Adams. The Leafs revolved around two players, center Syl Apps, Sr., and goalie Walter "Turk" Broda. Apps was big, fast, clean and durable, literally the All-Canadian Boy. The pudgy Broda often appeared too clumsy to be efficient, but he was at his best in the clutch. Their leading goal scorer was an exciting shooter named Gordie Drillon, and their defense was anchored by a pair of behemoths, Wilfred "Bucko" McDonald and Rudolph "Bingo" Kampman.

How the Red Wings managed to clamber up to the finals remained a mystery to those who had not followed Jack Adams' club closely in the last months of the season. True, the Wings did finish a distant fifth, 15 points behind the Maple Leafs, and were nearly ousted in the first playoff round by the Canadiens. But Detroit-watchers knew that the Red Wings had jelled in the last month from an inept, loosely coordinated team into a crisp winner. They proved it by upsetting the Bruins two games to none in the Stanley Cup semifinals. Utilizing brusing defensemen such as Jimmy Orlando and Jack Stewart, they intimidated the enemy; and practicing a completely new offensive technique — the Detroit forwards would skim the puck into the opposition zone and then race after it rather than pass their way in — they befuddled the traditional-minded foe.

"We may not be the greatest hockey club in the world," said Adams, "but we're loaded with fighting heart. And if there's anything that wins championships, it's just that!"

Despite the obvious superiority of the Leafs — on paper — a subtle air of anxiety trickled forth from parts of the Toronto camp. It was due partly to the Leafs' continuous inability to win the Stanley Cup as well as a suspicion that the Red Wings had the equipment to go all the way. Coach Day himself betrayed a certain anxiety when he labeled the Red Wings "a bunch of hoodlums." Major Conn Smythe, who had completed training and was preparing to leave Canada with his army group for Europe, surveyed the scene and delivered an uncharacteristically gloomy view of the series even before it had begun.

"Don't underestimate this Detroit club," warned Smythe. "They can skate, and they're going to run at us. Unless we match them check for check and stride for stride, we're going to be in trouble."

Right from the opening face-off, Adams sent his speedy skaters on their mission: Toss the puck in and dash after it, forecheck the Leafs into making mistakes. "It was not pretty hockey," said Stanley Cup historian Henry Roxborough, "but it was effective."

It was so effective that the normally poised Toronto skaters fumbled their way around the rink like battle-weary warriors. The Red Wings' harassment tactics worked on two levels: physical and mental. Tough Bob Goldham bled all the way to the bench after being clobbered by a stick to the head. Don "the Count" Grosso scored twice for Detroit, and the jubilant Red Wings skated off with a 3-2 upset triumph.

Anticipating his imminent departure for Europe, Major Smythe walked into the silent Leafs dressing room and sensed despair wherever he turned.

"I'm worried about this club," he told his aide Frank Selke. "It's going to be quite a job for Hap to straighten them out."

But the Maple Leafs were only one game down in a best-of-seven series, and they had lost by only one goal. Surely the next match, at Maple Leaf Gardens on April 7, would revitalize them. But it didn't. Before the second game had even started, manager Adams disregarded the cautionary policy adapted by his colleagues and openly predicted that his Red Wings would win the Stanley Cup in six games. Nothing that happened in the second game indicated that he was wrong, except the chance that Detroit might require fewer games than six.

Toronto fans were transfixed as they watched the Red Wings skate away with a 4-2 win. Grosso again scored twice, and teammates Mud Bruneteau and Jim Brown each tallied once. The beleaguered Leafs were able to get scores from Sweeney Schriner and Wally Stanowski, but the big guns of Apps and Drillon were strangely silent. Even worse, the usually reliable Bucko McDonald was proving to be especially vulnerable on defense when the Detroiters tried their new skate-and-run style.

On April 9 Motor City fans flocked to Olympia Stadium with glee to see whether what they had heard and read about their club was on the level. At first they thought it all was a joke. Toronto's Lorne Carr put two shots past goalie Johnny Mowers in no time at all, and the Leafs appeared to be in control for the first time in the series. Then the Wings skimmed the puck into the Toronto zone, and the Leafs backliners began falling over themselves trying to keep up with the Detroit sprinters. Before the period had ended, Gerry Brown and Joe Carveth had been set up for scores by Detroit defenseman Eddie Bush. The fact that center Sid Abel had retired with a badly bruised cheek seemed to inspire them to even greater efforts.

Bush proceeded to organize goals by Pat McReavy and Syd Howe; then he added one himself, and the underdog Detroiters suddenly found themselves favoured to capture the playoffs in an incredible four straight games. It was easy to understand the logic behind such talk. The usually reliable Drillon had been completely defused and had gone for seven playoff games without scoring. Needled by Bush and Orlando, Broda played his worst game of the series, and McDonald, the former Red Wing, was skating in mud on the Toronto defense. "You got the idea," wrote Vern DeGeer in the Toronto *Globe and Mail*, "that it was over but for the shouting."

Certainly everyone in Toronto thought so, and they heaped their abuse on coach Hap Day. "Smythe never should have allowed (coach) Dick Irvin to go to Montreal," said one fan. "Day can't handle this club."

And so it went. "They hooted Day's name," wrote Canadian writer Ron McAllister, "and told him to go home. He'd never been a player or a coach or a referee; he was just a stumblebum who didn't know anything."

Quitting in the face of defeat had never been Day's style, and he was not about to start. He coolly pondered the situation, seeking answers to the question of why his machine wasn't functioning the way it should. At last he thought he had the solution, but to be sure he phoned Smythe, who was stationed in Petawawa, Ontario. Conn endorsed the plan, as did Selke, although it was very possibly the most daring plan ever tried in a championship sports series any-where.

Day benched his ace scorer Gordie Drillon and his veteran defenseman Bucko McDonald. That in itself was startling enough, but Hap then revealed that they would be replaced by the most unlikely players imaginable. Drillon's substitute was Don Metz, kid brother of Nick Metz, who had scored only two goals all season and who had not played for about two weeks. McDonald was replaced by raw rookie, Ernie Dickens, who had played only 10 NHL games in his life.

In Detroit the move was interpreted as panic of the highest order. Every correspondent covering the series predicted a quick demise for the Toronto club, and a record 13,694 fans turned out to see the Red Wings do the honours. Apart from the dramatic bench-ing of Drillon and McDonald, Day attempted to explore all avenues of hope, including a letter he had received from a 14-year-old-girl.

Just before the game, Day walked into the Toronto dressing room and read the letter to his players. The young girl expressed her conviction that the Leafs really were capable of rallying to win the Stanley Cup. Somehow her belief actually inspired as hard-bitten a warrior as Day, and when he read the letter he oozed with such emotion that the Toronto players were similarly affected. A few seconds after Day had finished his reading, the old pro, Sweeney Schriner, clambered off his bench and said, "Don't worry about this one, Skipper, we'll win this one for the little girl." Then Billy Taylor shouted, "We're not licked yet!"

First Mud Brunetearu and then Sid Abel scored for the Red Wings, and with the game more than half over, Detroit held a commanding 2-0 lead. Mowers seemed to have the Red Wings' net boarded up for the night, and the fans in the Olympia could almost taste the Stanley Cup champagne. There was only one problem — the Maple Leafs forgot to quit.

Toronto needed one goal to ignite their frozen attack, and they finally gto it at 13:54 of the middle period when Bob Davidson took relays from Pete Langelle and Johnny McCreedy to beat Mowers. They were beginning to warm up and within two minutes they were hot. Taylor moved the puck to Schriner, who lateralled to Lorne Carr. Carr brought the score to 2-2, and it stayed that way through the end of the second period.

The Leafs' rally seemed to arouse the Red Wings to new strength in the third period, and despite Broda's courageous display, Carl Liscombe lifted Detroit into the lead again at 4:18 of the third. The screams of delight that reverberated off the walls of Olympia were frightening, because the fans believed that Liscombe's goal had applied the coup de grace to Hap Day's stunned skaters. But the Leafs possessed a persistence that would not tolerate defeat. Before the fans had calmed themselves over Liscombe's goal, Apps roared into Red Wing territory and delivered a smoking shot that beat Mowers. Then with 7:15 remaining in the period, Apps and Don Metz collaborated on passes to Nick Metz, who fooled the Detroit goalie. Broda held fast, and Toronto pulled off an astonishing 4-3 triumph. The first pressure of the choke had taken place.

The realization that they had come so close to the Stanley Cup and then allowed it to elude them had a disturbing effect on several Detroit players even before the final buzzer sounded. This inability to accept defeat was to have a far-reaching effect on the Red Wings and their Stanley Cup future.

Not long after Nick Metz had scored what was to be the game's winning goal, Wings defenseman Eddie Wares was handed a misconduct penalty by referee Mel Harwood. Instead of accepting the decision, Wares ignored Harwood's command and then insulted the official by handing him a hot-water bottle he obtained from the Detroit bench. Wares eventually skated to the penalty box, but not before Harwood had added a $50 fine to his sentence.

By then Jack Adams was livid, and he virtually exploded when Harwood gave Detroit another penalty for having too many men on the ice. Grosso was designated to antagonize Harwood, dropping his gloves and stick in front of the embattled referee. Harwood replied with a $25 fine.

The game finally continued to its conclusion, and all would have been well had Adams not decided to resume hostilities with the referee. Linemen Don McFayden and Sammy Babcock intervened, accompanied by the local police. One spectator taking all this in with consummate interest was NHL president Frank Calder. Calder fined Wares and Grosso $100 each, and Adams was suspended indefinitely.

As the teams returned to Toronto for the fifth game, at Maple Leaf Gardens on April 14, speculation mounted over Day's decision about Drillon and McDonald. Benching the veterans for one game was all right, but surely he wasn't going to try it again.

Day daringly answered the question a day before the game when he announced that he had still another ploy up his sleeve. He was promoting 19-year-old left wing Gaye Stewart to the Maple Leafs, although the rookie was less than a year out of junior hockey. Stewart was to replace Hank Goldup, a three-year NHL veteran.

Few could interpret precisely what effect Adams' suspension would have on the Red Wings. The Detroit high command decided that veteran Ebbie Goodfellow, who was no longer useful as a player, would coach the team in Adams' absence. The question was whether Detroit could recapture the momentum lost at Olympia or whether Day's unique experiment would work again.

The answer was supplied by the chief subject in the experiment, Don Metz. Metz scored a three-goal hat trick, driving the Leafs to a 9-3 shellacking of the Wings. Thus Toronto was down only three games to two, but the sixth game was slated for Olympia Stadium, and the Red Wings were ready to do anything to settle the issue on their home rink.

Led by Count Grosso and Sid Abel, the Detroiters mounted assault after assault in the first period. Their repeated shots seemed to zero in on Broda like tracer bullets, but he was more than equal to the occasion. When Grosso and Abel failed, coach Goodfellow tried to steal a page from Day's battle plan by sending out rookies Gus Giesebrecht and Doug McCaig. But they were not in the class of Don Metz and Ernie Dickens.

Broda's defiant stand in the first period deflated the Red Wings, and before the second period was 15 seconds old, Don Metz had done it again; a quick shot put Toronto in the lead, and it was followed by goals from Bob Goldham and Billy Taylor. The Leafs, who only a week earlier were teetering on the brink of elimination, had pulled themselves into a 3-3 tie in the series.

One Detroit spectator hurled a dead fish on the ice late in the game. "That dead fish," wrote Toronto writer Ed Fitkin, "seemed to be symbolic of Detroit fans' reaction to the collapse of their Red Wings."

The collapse had begun with Wares' and Grosso's tantrums

late in the fourth game, and it was furthered by Adams' attack on referee Harwood. "The wild outbursts," said hockey historian Roxborough, "did not help the morale of the Detroit players, and neither did the loss of their coach, who had to be replaced by a less experienced leader."

Still, the Red Wings, like the Maple Leafs had one more chance. The final game was played on the night of April 18, 1942 at Maple Leaf Gardens, where 16,240 spectators, the largest crowd in Canadian hockey history up to that point, came to see what fabric made up the Maple Leafs. They remembered the collapses of the past, and they wondered if it would happen again.

It certainly looked as though the Leafs would blow the duke again as they had in the past. Syd Howe put Detroit ahead, 1-0, and Toronto's attack suddenly fizzled, as it had in the first three games of the set. At one point goalie Mowers blunted the Toronto shots with his team two men short, and Detroit skated out for the third period guarding the 1-0 lead.

The Leafs needed a break, and they got it early in the third period when referee Bill Chadwick whistled Jimmy Orlando into the penalty box for two minutes. Coach Day sent the Schriner line out for the power play instead of Apps and the Metz brothers. "Sweeney was a big man," wrote Charles Coleman, "a fast skater and very nimble in his play."

Never was Schriner more nimble than he was in front of the Detroit net with his Maple Leafs on the brink of defeat. Sweeney awaited the pass, but had to turn his back to the cage. He did just that and rapped the puck past the startled Mowers to tie the score. The Maple Leafs were alive again!

Spectators crumpled programs in excitement; others leaned so far forward in their seats that they jammed their knees into the backs of those in the rows ahead of them. Everyone waited and hoped for the moment when Toronto could pull the string that would drop Detroit out of contention. But they worried about the Red Wings' propensity for coming from behind.

In the next two minutes the Red Wing forwards attempted to puncture the Maple Leafs' blue-line corps, but Day's "substitutes' came through nobly. Rookies Ernie Dickens and Bob Goldham would not be breached, and Don Metz checked zealously on the forward line.

A whistle was blown, and Day changed squads. He sent young center Pete Langelle on left wing with veteran Bob Davidson and Johnny McCreedy on the right side. Immediately they stormed into Red Wing ice with McCreedy leading the way with a shot on

Mowers. The Detroit goalie moved far out of his cage to deflect the drive, but the puck rebounded back into play, and Mowers was stranded away from the gaping net. In a desperate lunge the Detroit defense tried to cover Mowers' abandoned net, but Langelle pounced on the puck like a leopard seizing his prey and smacked it into the cage.

When the thunderous roar of the audience had diminished, Turk Broda knew that it was his game to win. The Maple Leafs were closer to the Stanley Cup than they had been in 10 years. Joe Carveth, Carl Liscombe and Gerry Brown of Detroit's first line tested the Turk, but Broda displayed the brand of goaltending that was to earn him a reputation as the most dependable money goalie in NHL history. After one sortie Turk punted the puck ahead to his defense as Schriner picked up speed at center ice. Sweeney took the pass and scored for the second time in the game. With less than five minutes to play, Toronto was ahead, 3-1.

One man more than any of the thousands in the arena fixed his eyes on the clock as the Maple Leafs battled to retain the lead. It was Conn Smythe, who had been granted permission by his army superiors to leave the Petawawa military base in order to watch his team in their most critical battle since he organized the Toronto hockey club. To Smythe the seconds seemed like hours as the hands on the clock moved toward the finish.

Try as they might, the Red Wings could not secure a bridgehead in Toronto territory. The clock began to tick off the final minute of play, and the 16,240 spectators helped it along with a second-by second chant until they recited the final "five ... four ... three ... two ... one!!" And the bell sounded ending the series.

In his book *Turk Broda of the Leafs*, Ed Fitkin described the last seconds: "Pandemonium broke loose on the ice and in the stands at the final bell. Every player on the Leaf bench leaped over the boards and rushed out on the ice to grab and hug a teammate, while the crowd roared with ecstasy of the moment . . . the moment they had waited ten long years to witness.

"Broda, grinning and whooping, was mobbed by every Leaf at the final bell. Young Bob Goldham, who had been a great playoff performer, hugged him enthusiastically and said: 'Guess we showed 'em, Slip! You old sonofagun, you were terrific!' Probably the most excited man on the ice was Captain Syl Apps. Blood streaming from a cut down the side of his nose, Syl dashed to the Leaf bench and said: 'C'mon, Conny and get the Cup.'"

Never before had a team lost the first three games of a Stanley Cup series and then pulled itself together to win the next four and the championship. "That was a night I shall long remember," said broadcaster Foster Hewitt, who had seen more hockey games than anyone in the world. "It was a thrilling tribute to hockey's outstanding comebacks, a team with the fight to turn a rout into a triumph."

Conn Smythe, who had so often leaped over the sideboards to assail an enemy player or referee, this time vaulted the timbers and marched proudly to center ice, where NHL president Frank Calder awaited him and the players congratulated one another; suddenly Goldham realized that his coach was not among them.

Hap Day, the man so bitterly reviled by spectators and the press during the early days of the finals, was watching the proceedings from the throng at center ice. The moment Day stepped on the rink his appearance touched off a tumultuous ovation, as if the Maple Leafs had just won the Stanley Cup again.

For a time it seemed as though the cheering would never stop. The Leafs' dressing room was surrounded by thousands of well-wishers long into the night. It was as though 10 years of frustration were finally being released by the Toronto hockey enthusiasts. The celebration didn't really end until late the next day, after a reception at the Royal York Hotel in downtown Toronto.

For months after the Stanley Cup finals hockey experts analyzed the arresting Toronto triumph, trying to ascertain precisely what had brought about victory when defeat seemed so imminent.

One theory had it that Red Wings manager Jack Adams had "blown" the series after the fourth game when he erupted at referee Mel Harwood and invited suspension for the remainder of the playoffs. Adams, of course, was able to transmit his strategy to acting coach Ebbie Goodfellow, but his eruption seemed to have a debilitating effect on morale in the Detroit camp. "If the Red Wings had maintained their composure," wrote one critic, "there is no question that they would have kept the edge on Toronto and won the Stanley Cup. In big-league hockey a 'cool' club often can defeat a superior team that panics, as the Red Wings did in April, 1942."

By contrast, Hap Day had remained cool. His awesome benching of Gordie Drillon and Bucko McDonald bore that rare touch of genius, as was proved by Ernie Dickens and Don Metz, the replacements who performed so well under fire. "We couldn't have won the Cup," said captain Apps, "if the Skipper didn't have faith in us. He won the Cup more than anybody."

Great Vintage Players

1. Johnny Bower — played to age 46.
2. Gordie Howe — played to age 52! Only player ever to play on same team with sons, Marty and Mark (Houston Aeros in WHA, then with Mark on Whalers in NHL, 1979-80).
3. Doug Harvey — played to age 45.
4. Glenn Hall — played to age 40.
5. Jacques Plante — played to age 46.
6. Les Binkley — was 32-year old rookie goalie with Pittsburgh in 1967-68. Retired at 40.

The Trivia question is, who was supposed to succeed Gordie Howe on the Detroit Red Wings Production Line? Tom Webster — although the transition wasn't too smooth.

The All-Dirtiest, Toughest Team

Eddie Shore (NHL, 1926-40)
No big league hockey player came closer to killing an opponent in a game than Shore, a Boston Bruins defenseman who had 978 stitches laced over 80 wounds on his torso.

Shore almost killed Toronto Maple Leafs forward Ace Bailey during a game at Boston Garden in 1933. During a particularly bloody battle, Shore checked Bailey, a generally peaceful man, from behind. Bailey's head struck the ice and he was carried off with a skull fracture. For several days Bailey teetered between life and death in a Boston hospital. He eventually recovered, but never played hockey again.

The fact that Shore wantonly charged a peaceful man like Bailey — apparently Shore mistook Bailey for another Leaf — while Bailey had his back turned and was completely unprepared for the blow, and damn near killed him, puts Shore at the top of this list.

Shore, an eventual Hall of Famer and admittedly one of the best defenseman ever to play the game professionally, got his come-uppance years later when he started a fight with Phil Watson of the Rangers. Watson's teammate Murray Patrick intervened and flattened Shore for the count. Patrick had once been amateur heavyweight champion of Canada.

Ted Lindsay (NHL, 1944-65)
Lindsay was equally potent with his stick or dukes, depending on the occasion. During a game between Boston and Lindsay's Detroit Red Wings in 1951, Lindsay and Bill Ezinicki of the Bruins duelled with their sticks and then exchanged punches. Ezinicki lost one tooth and needed 19 stitches to close assorted wounds.

"It was a case of self-survival," said Lindsay. "He had hit me over the head after the whistle and cut me at the hairline, so I tapped him back. Then he dropped his stick and his gloves, so we ended up in a fight."

Lindsay's flailing stick was used as often as an intimidating device as it was for scoring. He is personally credited with running at least one player out of the NHL with his menacing tactics. Some critics charged that Lindsay was tough only when his powerful linemate Gordie Howe was around.

"I interpret toughness with ability to back up any situation which may arise," former Montreal Canadien manager Frank Selke, Sr., once said. "I cannot place Lindsay in this category because he is mean and quick with his stick, but cannot back it up with his dukes!'

The majority opinion had it the other way. Former Toronto Maple Leafs president Stafford Smythe recalled of Lindsay: "He is tough because he is dirty!"

Leo Labine (NHL, 1951-62)

As a member of the Boston Bruins, Labine made a policy of head-hunting the superstars, especially Maurice "Rocket" Richard. He nearly killed Richard one night, blindsiding him with a combination knee to the groin and crosscheck to the head. Richard was carried unconscious from the ice but later returned to score the winning goal.

Labine could fight with his fists but like Lindsay was notorious for his quick stick, usually waved around an opponent's mouth. "I don't know anybody who likes to eat wood," said Labine, "unless he's a beaver."

Unlike many marauders, Labine was as terrifying with his tongue as he was with his stick. One night a piqued Rocket Richard jammed a butt end of his stick into Labine's ribs. Leo barked: "Look, Rocket, you've got thirty-two teeth. Do you want to try for sixteen?"

Labine had several bloody run-ins, parting the scalp of Chicago's Gus Mortson with his stick, trading punches with tough Tod Sloan, and fencing with Richard.

In his old age Labine mellowed. One night in Toronto Eric Nesterenko, then of the Maple Leafs, broke a hockey stick over Labine's head. "You shouldn't do such things," said Labine. "You'll get a penalty!"

Gordie Howe (NHL, 1946-71, 1979-80; WHA, 1973-79)

Dozens of players, coaches and managers have branded Howe as the greatest and dirtiest player of all time. With surgical precision Howe used his stick blade against the most formidable opponents. Once he nearly removed Ranger defenseman Lou Fontinato's ear. Another time he bashed in Fontinato's nose. "Howe," Phil Watson, ex-Rangers coach and Vancouver Blazers manager once said, "gets away with murder. Cross-checks, high-sticks, the works. He's been doing it for years."

Former teammate Ted Lindsay was one of the few — besides Gordie himself — to defend the Howe style. According to Lindsay it was less than fair to call Howe a dirty hockey player.

"What is dirty?" said Lindsay. "If dirty means protecting yourself, Gordie is dirty. When you're the best, you can't let the other team take chunks of flesh out of you. In other words Gordie was protecting himself."

When Gordie played in the NHL a poll among managers placed him at the top of the list among "toughest players in the league." More than a decade later, in 1973-74, WHA bosses said the same thing.

Fernie Flaman (NHL, 1944-61)

A mean, highly competent defenseman, Flaman once nearly took Ranger Andy Bathgate's eye out with a stick, and another time, almost skewered Camille Henry of the Rangers. "Flaman," said Henry, "was absolute murder to play against."

Although Flaman had a Milquetoast look about him, more than one NHL tough guy confided, "I wouldn't want to come face-to-face with him in a fight."

Flaman rarely lost his cool, but once former Red Wings coach Jimmy Skinner antagonized him from the bench. Flaman skated over to the Detroit bench and smacked Skinner in the face.

One night in a playoff game against the Canadiens, Flaman lifted Henri Richard of Montreal off the ice with his two hands as Richard was in flight, and then hurled the Canadien back on the ice in one motion.

"Flaman" wrote Jack Zanger in *Sport* magazine, "was the most dangerous Bruin to tangle with."

Washington Capitals manager Milt Schmidt, who once coached Flaman in Boston, called him "a solid bodychecker who was at his best when things were rough."

Edouard "Newsy" Lalonde (NHL, 1917-1922)

According to one veteran hockey writer, Lalonde "spilled enough corpuscles to gratify any blood bank on the continent."

Prior to formation of the NHL, Lalonde played in various Canadian pro leagues. His clashes with "Bad" Joe Hall, who later became a teammate on the Canadiens, were studies in jungle brutality, but Newsy never reserved his venom for Hall.

Once, Newsy bashed Hall across the head with his stick, opening an eight-stitch wound. The next time they met, Hall crashed Lalonde so hard Newsy required 10 stitches for his wounds.

In another match, Lalonde hit Odie Cleghorn viciously enough to inspire Odie's brother Sprague to charge across the rink and smash Newsy across the forehead with his stick. The blow just barely missed Lalonde's eye, and he required 12 stitches to close that gaping wound.

"Without question," said the late Dick Beddoes, then with the Toronto *Globe and Mail*, "Lalonde could buckle a swash with any ruffian alive."

Tony Leswick (NHL, 1945-58)

If you were to take the trouble to ask each NHL player during the late '40s or early '50s for his opinion of little Tony Leswick, the reply would be "pest" or any number of synonyms thereof.

Ted Lindsay, who was Leswick's teammate after Tony was traded from the Rangers to the Red Wings in 1941, like to greet Leswick with the observation, "You little toad!"

Leswick was little (five feet, six inches; 160 pounds) and he was tough. He usually took on bigger men and frequently lost but always came back for more. Once, rugged Howie Meeker of the Maple Leafs grappled with Leswick, lifted Tony about the waist, and dispatched him to the ice with a thud. The unconscious Ranger was taken to the infirmary, revived, and eventually returned to the game with a turbanlike bandage swathing his head.

"Tough Tony," as New York fans liked to call him, also was dirty, nasty, sneaky; you name it, that's what they called him. "He was the chippiest bloke in the league," said former teammate Don Raleigh.

Toronto defenseman Garth Boesch put it another way: "Leswick would get under your arms and between your legs. He'd annoy the life out of you."

His style was similar to Leo Labine's. He'd use his tongue as effectively as his stick. "Tony would get up close and laugh at his opponents," said former teammate Nick Mickoski. "He'd do anything to get under their skin. Once, when I played against him, we were good friends. I let up for a second and then wham! He knocked me right out of the play."

Some of Leswick's more notable targets were Jean Beliveau, Bill Ezinicki and Maurice "Rocket" Richard. The Rocket once bluntly summed up his feeling about Leswick's decorum this way: "I have nothing good to say about Tony Leswick."

Carol "Cully" Wilson (NHL, 1919-27)

The post-World War I era produced a large number of skaters who would think nothing of shoving a stick down an enemy's throat and often tried it. Cully Wilson was one of them.

In 1925, when Wilson was playing for the Calgary Tigers, he cross-checked Dick Irvin's teeth into his tongue. When Irvin recovered he knocked Wilson cold, using his stick as a bludgeon.

Wilson's most memorable battle has long been regarded as hockey's most private fight and symbolized the ferocity of the old-time game.

It was in 1917 and Wilson had been feuding with Cy Denneny, a star with the Ottawa Senators. Their running battle had extended through a whole season without noticeable result, and both players were thirsting for blood.

They realized that a full-scale brawl during a regular-season game might be damaging to their respective teams as well as bring suspensions upon themselves, so they waited until an exhibition All-Star game was to be played on non-NHL turf in Cleveland.

"The two of them knew," said hockey historian Bill Roche, "that they would be free from fines and suspensions, since the NHL had no supervision over the game."

The match was played in Cleveland's old Elysium rink, and according to witnesses, it was one of the most vicious ever to take place on or off the ice. Hall of Famer Frank Nighbor, who was there at the time and who had played in hundreds of games, called it "the hardest and longest fight" he had seen.

"Neither the rink nor the city police were inclined to interfere," said Roche. "The result was a draw in what was hockey's most thoroughly private bout."

No, that's not the latest style in hockey jerseys. But it is Ranger defenseman Brad Park being escorted off the ice by linesman Pat Shetler after being stripped in a brawl with the Canadiens

THE ALL-TIME WORST TEAMS

1. Philadelphia Quakers

Prior to expansion, a line in the NHL Record Book succinctly said it all about the worst team in major-league hockey: Fewest wins, one season— 4, Philadelphia Quakers, 1930-31, 44 — game schedule.

It was the height of irony that Phildelphia's Quakers were owned by a man who almost never lost, former lightweight champion Benny Leonard. Unfortunately for Benny, the Quakers made up for all of his non-ice triumphs and then some.

In fact the Quakers had a legacy of losses even before their opening face-off! Leonard originally bought the club in 1928-29 when it was the Pittsburgh Pirates. Not only did the Pirates lose games with ease, they also lost fans, and in October, 1930, the NHL approved Leonard's request to move the team to Philadelphia.

"The Quakers," said an overenthused Leonard, "are to ice hockey what the Athletics are to baseball."

Well, not quite. The A's were then the World Champions. The Quakers had yet to step on the ice. When they did they slipped and went right on slipping for the rest of the season.

Their goaltender, Joe Miller, was mediocre; the defense was virtually nonexistent, and the only scoring threats were Hib Milks and Gerry Lowrey. All of these minuses jelled on opening night, November 11, 1930, against the Rangers. Philadelphia lost 3-0.

After losing their first three games, the Quakers began to improve, although it was short lived. They tied Ottawa, 2-2, and then finally won their first game on November 25, 1930, defeating Toronto 2-1. Almost immediately though, disaster piled on disaster. The Quakers failed to win a single game from November 29, 1930, to January 10, 1931, setting a league record — 15 straight losses — that still stands.

The Quakers literally could do nothing right, not even get hurt. One night Philadelphia defenseman Stan Crossett was brutally sandwiched between a pair of Detroit defensemen and knocked flying into the air. Crossett was hit so hard he was unconscious before he even hit the ice. Ordinarily, a penalty might have been called against the perpetrators, but with typical Quakers' luck the unconscious Crossett got the penalty. He had accidentally hit one of the Detroit players with his stick as he flew through the air. The referee gave Crossett a five-minute penalty for drawing blood while he was stretched out unconscious on the ice!

Inept as they were, the Quakers never shied away from a good fight. They lost 8-0 to Boston on Christmas Day, 1930, but came out even in a series of intense brawls that caused officials to send for a battalion of Boston police.

The Quakers scored a moral victory when they returned to Boston for a rematch with the Bruins. This time they held the vastly superior home club to a 3-3 tie. Meanwhile, Leonard was losing money faster than his Quakers were losing hockey games. When the Montreal Canadiens offered him a first-rate defenseman for only $5,000, Benny said thanks-but-no-thanks; NHL hockey in Philadelphia was, for the time being, doomed.

In their final match, the Quakers tied the Canadiens, 4-4, and then disbanded. And rightly so. They had won four games, lost 36, and tied four. Major-league hockey has never suffered so terrible a team since.

2. New York Rangers

Prior to America's entry into World War II, the New York Rangers had fused one of the most powerful clubs the NHL had known. Featuring such high scorers as Bryan Hextall, Sr., Lynn Patrick and Phil Watson, the Rangers won the Stanley Cup in 1940 and the Prince of Wales Trophy (first place) during the 1941-42 season.

But armed forces enlistments drained the New York sextet of its best players, and when the 1942-43 campaign began, the Rangers were but a shade of their former powerful selves. In fact not only were they bad, they were ludicrous.

Even before the season began, events were moving from the ridiculous to the absurd. With goalies Jim Henry and Chuck Rayner already in the Canadian army, the Rangers did not even have a single regular netminder with whom to open camp.

Both club president Lester Patrick and manager Frank Boucher sent an SOS to Ranger scouts advising them to find a goaltender, any goaltender! The birddogs took the advice literally, and when training camp finally opened in Winnipeg a young man named Steve Buzinski skated between the pipes for the Rangers. Never has there been a more unlikely looking goaltender.

"He was a skinny, scrawny guy," said Boucher, "a little fellow who was the most bowlegged goaltender I ever saw. You could easily shoot a puck between the space created by his legs and his goalie pads."

It took a few days for Boucher to realize just how bad Buzinski was. "Not only was he not a big-league goaltender," the manager lamented, "but he was not a big-league wartime goaltender."

Perhaps the most bizarre aspect of Buzinski's brief NHL career was Lester Patrick's affection for him. Lester, hockey's "Silver Fox," was regarded as a superb critic of playing talent. And Patrick thought Buzinski was good, too. "I think you'll be pleasantly surprised with him," Patrick assured a dubious Boucher.

But the only surprises involved Buzinski's repertoire of strange tricks. There was the night at Maple Leaf Gardens when Steve was knocked to the ice by a Toronto player. "From the bench," said Boucher, "I could see Steve flat on his back. Then he was in a sitting position. Then he was flat on his back again. Lynn Patrick came skating from the goal-mouth pileup to our bench, and he was laughing so hard he was shaking.

"'You'll never believe this,' said Lynn. 'We thought Steve had been knocked out. We were yelling for a penalty to Davidson for high-sticking. Davidson said he didn't hit him. It was the puck. He got hit in the head with the puck. That's when Steve, lying there cold as a mackerel, sat straight up and said to the referee, 'That's a damn lie. He high-sticked me,' and fell flat on his back again with his eyes closed."

After six games and 55 goals scored against him, Buzinski could see the handwriting on the dressing-room wall. He was finished as a Ranger regular.

As a team, the Rangers were so bad that none of Buzinski's replacements made much of a difference. They won only 11 of 50 games and finished sixth among the six teams. It appeared that the New Yorkers could not possibly get worse, but they did! A year later they won only six out of 50 games!

Patrick began to think Boucher's coaching might be the problem, but Lester got the answer on January 23, 1944, when Boucher took the night off to attend his brother's funeral. Patrick took Boucher's place behind the bench that night in Detroit's Olympia Stadium and played a part in one of the most humiliating defeats ever in the NHL. With Ken "Tubby" McAuley in the nets for New York, the Red Wings scored 15 consecutive goals and won the game 15-0.

The game set records for (a) most consecutive goals, one team, one game; (b) most points, one team, one game; (C) most goals, one team, one period; and (d) most points, one team, one period.

"I think," said Boucher, "this particular game persuaded him that there was something even more fundamentally wrong with the team than my coaching."

The only thing wrong with the Rangers was World War II. After hostilities ended, the soldiers came home, and by 1945-46 the Rangers were competitive again. By that time poor goalie McAuley had nearly been vulcanized by all the rubber that had hit him and never stayed around for the Rangers' renaissance.

"McAuley, bless his heart," said Boucher, "he should have been awarded the Croix de Guerre, if not the Victoria Cross, for bravery above and beyond the call of duty."

3.Chicago Blackhawks

In Chicago's very first year of NHL hockey, a curse purportedly was put on the Blackhawks that was to have long-lasting repercussions. It happened when club owner Major Frederic McLaughlin criticized his coach, Pete Muldoon, for not winning the Stanley Cup in their maiden season.

"You're crazy," shouted the incensed Muldoon at his boss. At which the Major handed his coach a pink slip and told him to find work elsewhere.

Muldoon stared down McLaughlin. "I'm not through with you," the just-fired coach reportedly warned the Major. "I'll hoodoo you. This club will never finish in first place."

Whether the events happened exactly as told is hardly relevant. What matters is that Muldoon's hex, or whatever it was, must have worked. Year after year, no matter how good the Blackhawks were, they never finished first as long as the Major was alive.

When McLaughlin died in 1944, the Blackhawks were a mediocre club on a treadmill to oblivion. Then things began to get worse. The Major was succeeded by his aide, Bill Tobin, who managed to do just about everything wrong that was possible with a good franchise.

He failed to build and maintain an adequate farm system. He lacked a comprehensive scouting program. His trading philosophy was medieval, and he had little rapport with his coaches. Otherwise, Tobin was a veritable hockey genius.

Naturally, it all came out in the standings. From the 1946-47 season through 1951-52, the Blackhawks finished last five times and fifth once. "I couldn't put the Blackhawks on the rink as my home team," said an NHL coach. "After seeing them once, everybody would stay as far away as they could get. Chicago must be the greatest hockey city in the country to keep on supporting them."

Chicago was a great hockey city — as great as the Blackhawks were terrible. Capacity crowds at mammoth Chicago Stadium were the rule, and that, in part, explains the front-office flops. "The management had it too easy for too long," said a Blackhawks' critic. "They knew that no matter how bad the team, the fans would show up. They became lax and didn't work at the job."

At the end of World War II, Chicago had the nucleus of a contender. Max and Doug Bentley were two of the best scorers in the NHL, and linemate Bill Mosienko was coming on strong. But they needed help, and that's where Tobin failed them. He failed to cultivate farm clubs in Western Canada, where the Blackhawks were extremely popular because the Bentleys came from Saskatchewan.

"We trained at Regina for the 1945-46 and 1946-47 seasons,"

said then Chicago coach Johnny Gottselig. "That gave us a foothold in the territory. Our club was tremendously popular in the area then. The Bentleys were the idols of Canadian youngsters in that section. 'We want to play where the Bents play' was a popular refrain.

"If the proper steps had been taken then, we could have cornered the whole West for amateur talent. But the next year the club moved the training site, and we missed our great chance. When we failed to press our advantage in the West, Detroit moved into the territory and wrapped it up."

One of Tobin's biggest blunders was the breakup of the famed Bentleys. Early in the 1947-48 season, he traded Max Bentley, hockey's greatest scorer of the day, to Toronto along with Cy Thomas for three forwards and two defensemen. Tobin not only relinquished high quality for quantity, but also demoralized Doug Bentley in the process. That the trade was an abject failure was underlined in the spring of 1947. The Blackhawks finished dead last while the Maple Leafs, led by Max Bentley, finished first and won the Stanley Cup.

Frequently, Tobin would sell players for cash, a move that inspired a rival to term it "the height of stupidity."

"He'd sell players for ten or fifteen thousand dollars, instead of trading them for the rights to promising youngsters," one NHL official said. "I told Tobin, 'You can't play thousand-dollar bills at those wing positions.'"

Tobin made one good move — he hired veteran center Sid Abel as player-coach in 1952. With Abel behind the bench and excellent goalkeeper Al Rollins between the pipes, the Blackhawks actually finished fourth in 1952-52. But it was just a mirage. A year later they were sixth again, winning only 12, tying seven, and losing 51 games. "That club," said Detroit hockey writer Tommy Devine, "was one of the weakest teams in NHL history."

The Blackhawks of that season were so bad that their leading scorer, Larry Wilson, scored only nine goals. Rollins was the only ray of hope, and he was buried under a barrage of rubber. Worse still, fans for the first time began staying away from Chicago Stadium by the thousands. Hard as it was to believe, the Blackhawks were close to folding their operation.

In September, 1952, Jim Norris and Arthur Wirtz purchased the club. They studied the mounting losses and had to make a decision — either quit hockey or pour millions into the franchise in the hopes of reviving it.

They decided to save the Blackhawks.

Tobin was shunted to an inconsequential front-office position and replaced by clever Tommy Ivan, who had coached the Red Wings to a couple of Stanley Cup triumphs.

Using Rollins and defenseman Bill Gadsby as a nucleus, Ivan began building. It took a while for Ivan to construct a farm system, but he did, and by 1958-59 the Blackhawks had climbed to third place. In 1961, led by Ivan discoveries Stan Mikita and Bobby Hull, they won the Stanley Cup. And in 1967 they actually broke the 40-year-old Muldoon jinx and finished in first place.

4. Quebec Nordiques

When it comes to bad teams, the Nordiques differ from their predecessors. They began their professional life in the World Hockey Association and graduated to the NHL in 1979. The coup that brought Peter and Anton Stastny to the NHL turned Quebec into a competitive team.

Les Nordiques reached the heights in 1983-84, when they recorded their highest season point total of 94 and a berth in the Division finals against Montreal. Quebec lost that series but put together a 91-point season and a trip to the Conference finals against Philadelphia in 1984-85, only to lose in seven games. The Nordiques finally reached a Divisional first place with a 92-point season in 1985-86, but once again lost in the Division semi-finals. From that season on the Nordiques started slipping drastically in points, hitting their all-time low a dismal 31 points in the 1989-90 season.

Precisely what went wrong with Quebec is a matter of conjecture. Some believe the trouble began with the firing of Michel Bergeron. A succession of coaches did little to relieve the problem. Among those who tried to resurrect the Nordiques were Ron Lapointe, Jean Perron and Dave Chambers. The club missed the playoffs for five straight years and some cynics believe that there was little motivation to produce a winner since the club was selling out on a regular basis. It was a measure of Quebec's bad luck that even when the Nordiques drafted a prize such as Eric Lindros, they still finished last in the Adams division and, naturally, Lindros wouldn't report!

Quebec's problems were particularly hard on its goalies. Les Nordiques used four goaltenders in the 1988-89 season, producing a poor 4.24 goals against average, then changed to a staggering seven goalies for 1989-90, leading the league with a whopping 5.05 goals against average.

After finishing the 1988-89 season with a somewhat respectable 61 points, the Nordiques floundered to a 12-win, 61-loss, and seven-tie record, an NHL low for the decade of the '80s. How and why had the Nordiques become so bad, so quickly?

In the 1989-90 season, the Nords leading scorer was Joe Sakic, who produced 102 points in his sophomore year, to land him in the top 10 in scoring. But the next leading scorer on the team was defenseman Michel Petit, with a total of 36 points! In a span of one season the Nordiques lost Peter Stastny, Walt Poddubny, Jeff Brown and Michel Goulet — the top four scorers on the Nordiques the previous season, ahead of Joe Sakic who was fifth.

The Nordiques set many club records that season and nearly every record highlighted the team's futility. They had the most losses (61), most home losses (26), most road losses (35), most goals aginst (407), fewest points (31), fewest home points (22), fewest road points (9), fewest wins (12), fewest home wins (8), longest winless streak (14), fewest road ties (1), fewest road goals (101), most home goals against (192), most road goals against (215), most power-play goals against (tied with 98).

5. Washington Capitals

By 1975 the NHL was in the midst of a bitter blood war with the World Hockey Association. Further diluting NHL talent was the fact that two new franchises were admitted to the NHL, Kansas City and Washington.

How bad were the Capitals? They were this bad. In 80 games under two coaches, Milt Schmidt and Tom McVie, the Caps had only 11 wins, 59 losses and 10 ties for 32 points. The leading scorer on this team was Nelson Pyatt who finished the season with only 26 goals and 23 assists, for 49 points, and a team-leading minus-56 rating. Their best goaltender that year was Bernie Wolfe, who had five wins, 23 losses, seven ties and a whopping 4.16 goals against average. McVie managed to make the most of a bad situation. McVie took command on December 30, 1975, when the club was 3-28-5. It took Tom 12 games in the big league before he won one. "But I bounced out of the Sheraton-Lanham every morning for the first three or four days," McVie recalls. "'Gentlemen,' I would say, 'I have these things planned for today. We'll do some two-on-ones, some three-on-ones . . . ' And I saw the looks on them like 'this guy is bleeping crazy.' I went on with it and they just leaned on their sticks and listened. Finally I asked if anybody had anything to say."

"'Why are we doing all this,' inquired defenseman Bob Paradise [who had become a Capital just in time to be in on the winless streak], 'when we know we're going to bleeping lose anyway?'

"'Well, then,' I said, 'why don't we all go to Mr. Pollin's [Caps owner] office and tell him we are disbanding the team?' Then I cooled down and told them they might as well get used to it; I'm not going to be any different."

In the fall of the 1976 season, hoping to improve on the dismal 1975-76 campaign, McVie took 60 people to camp at Hershey, Pennsylvania and worked them from six a.m. to midnight. He returned to Washington feeling he had picked the right twenty. "We've done our work," he said after the Caps had held Montreal to a 4-3 score, "and shoulda won it."

And then they didn't win for 42 days: 20 games without a victory.

"God," McVie said, as the winless streak rolled on, from October into December, "we've won two games. We could have done that without having a training camp. We coulda gone out and got drunk and won three or four, couldn't we?"

The Capitals remained a miserable, motley crew long after McVie's departure. They didn't straighten out until the 1982-83 season, when David Poile, then a rookie general manager, obtained Rod Langway, Doug Jarvis, Brian Engblom and Criag Laughlin from the Canadiens.

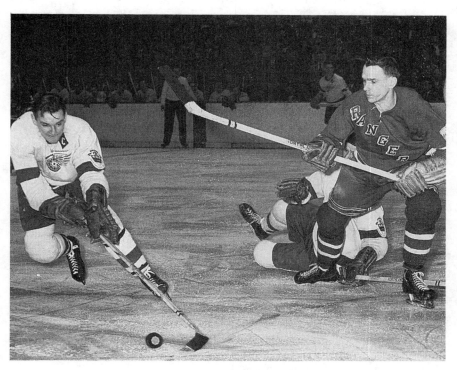

The player on the right was a pretty good NHL forward. But Reg Sinclair attained greater eminence as a business executive with Coca Cola. The famous one on the left is Red Wings' captain Sid Abel.

The Best Smiths in Hockey History

Goaltenders:

Billy (1971-89) — Los Angeles, New York Islanders — winner of four Stanley Cups, 3.17 goals against average.

Al (1965-81) — Toronto, Pittsburgh, Detroit, Buffalo, Hartford, Colorado — 3.46 average.

Gary "Suitcase" (1965-80) — Toronto, Oakland, California, Chicago, Vancouver, Minnesota, Washington, Winnipeg — 3.39 average.

Others:

Alex (1924-35) — Ottawa, Detroit, Boston, New York Americans — winner of one Cup (Ottawa '27); 443 games played.

Bobby (1978-) — Minnesota, Montreal — 1000+ games played, 1000+ points, one Cup.

Brad (1978-87) — Vancouver, Atlanta, Calgary, Detroit, Toronto — 222 games played, 591 penalty minutes.

Clint "Snuffy" (1936-47) — Rangers, Chicago — 483 games played; member of last Ranger Cup-winning team in 1940; two-time Lady Byng winner.

Dallas (1959-78) — Boston, New York Rangers — winner of two Cups (Boston '70, '72); 890 games played.

Floyd (1954-72) — Boston, Rangers, Detroit, Toronto, Buffalo — 550 games played.

Greg (1975-88) — California, Cleveland, Minnesota, Detroit, Washington — 829 games played; 1110 penalty minutes.

Hooley (1924-41) — Ottawa, Maroons, Boston, Americans — 719 games played; member of 1927 Ottawa Cup winner; Hall of Famer.

Rick (1968-81) — Boston, California, St. Louis, Detroit, Washington — winner of one Cup (Boston '70); 687 games played.

Sid (1946-58) — Toronto — 601 games played; two 30-goal seasons.

GOAL MAGAZINE'S 100 THINGS YOU NEVER KNEW ABOUT THE NHL

1. On December 9, 1941, Boston's game against Chicago was delayed for 28 minutes as players and fans at Boston Garden listened to President Franklin Delano Roosevelt announce to the nation that war had been declared.

2. Armand "Bep" Guidolin was the youngest player ever to play in the NHL, beginning his nine-year career in November of 1942 at age 16.

3. Frank Brimsek, hockey's "Mr. Zero," was the first to modify his stick hand glove so he could block shots with the back of his hand.

4. Willie O'Ree became the first black to play in the NHL on January 18, 1958.

5. Defenseman Ray Bourque is one of only two players (Wayne Gretzky is the other) to have been an all-star in each of his first 12 NHL seasons.

6. Goaltender Don Simmons was the second NHL goaltender to don a mask, following Montreal's Jacques Plante.

7. Right wing Jerry Toppazzini was the last regular-position player to tend goal in an NHL game, replacing an injured Don Simmons on October 6, 1960 in the last minute of a 4-1 loss to Detroit.

8. The Sabres of 1978-79 allowed only 201 goals-against, the lowest total since the NHL became a 22-team league.

9. The Sabres were named through a fan contest. There were five entries suggesting the name Sabres, a total of 13,000 entries suggested 1,047 different names. "Flying Zeppelins" and "Mugwumps" didn't make the final cut.

10. When the Sabres met the Flyers for the Stanley Cup in 1975, Game Three became known as the "fog game" because of the fog on-ice created by warm temperatures inside Buffalo's Memorial Auditorium. The game was stopped 11 times for fog breaks.

11. The Buffalo Sabres were the hosts when Wayne Gretzky broke the NHL's record for most goals in a season. He scored goal number 77 February 24, 1982; Don Edwards allowed the goal.

12. After moving to Calgary from Atlanta in 1980, the Flames played three seasons in the 7,242-seat Stampede Corral — perhaps the smallest arena in NHL history. Since 1983, the Flames have called the 20,132 seat Olympic Saddledome their home.

13. The name "Flames" was decided upon in 1972 by an Atlanta committee comprised of media representatives, and was based on the historical account of General Sherman's burning of Atlanta during the Civil War.

14. At five-feet, six inches, Theoren Fleury is the shortest NHL player to record a 50-goal season.

15. Goaltender Emile Francis wore a baseball style first baseman's mitt in a 1948 game against Detroit. The NHL approved the "trapper-style" glove a year later.

16. Steve Larmer became the NHL's iron man of the Nineties, finishing the 1991-92 season with a string of 800 consecutive games played (moving him into all-time third place, behind Doug Jarvis with 964 and Garry Unger with 914).

17. Chicago Stadium was the first to host an NHL matinee game, when Chicago downed Detroit 4-2 in a 1933 game that began at 3:30 p.m.

18. On March 16, 1941, coach Paul Thompson pulled goaltender Sam LoPresti for an extra attacker — the first time on record that the tactic was used in the NHL.

19. Detroit's Bill Quackenbush won the Lady Byng Trophy in 1949, playing all 60 games without incurring a penalty.

20. The Red Wings were originally called the Cougars; then the Falcons. They achieved their final name and the winged wheel insignia on their jerseys in 1932, when James Norris bought the club. Norris had played amateur hockey on a team which sported that insignia and were called the Winged Wheelers. Norris

decided that such a symbol would perfectly represent Detroit, which has the nickname of Motor City.

21. Former Detroit netminder Roger Crozier was the last Red Wing to win the Calder Memorial Trophy for Rookie of the Year (1965). He also became the first goaltender and first player on a Stanley Cup Losing team to win the playoff MVP award, the Conn Smythe Trophy (1966).

22. The late Terry Sawchuk holds the NHL record for career shutouts with 103. He posted 85 of those shutouts with the Red Wings; that number alone would place him third on the all-time list.

23. The Red Wings were the first major sports team to offer their fans a season-ticket plan. Initiated in 1933, Red Wings fans had the option of paying for their seats in five monthly installments.

24. The Oilers hold the record for the most goals scored in one season — 446 during the 1983-84 season.

25. Defenseman Kevin Lowe scored the first NHL goal in Oilers history on October 10, 1979 at Chicago. The first Oilers' hat trick was recorded by Blair McDonald on October 19, 1979 at home versus Quebec.

26. Joe Murphy was the first-ever collegiate player (Michigan State) chosen first overall in the NHL Entry Draft. Murphy was selected number one by the Detroit Red Wings in 1986.

27. Talk about unlikely: Wayne Gretzky took the Oilers' first NHL penalty, receiving two minutes for slashing at 5:19 of the first period of the Oilers' first NHL game (at Chicago, October 10, 1979).

28. Glen Sather is the only general manager the Oilers have had since they joined the NHL in 1979.

29. The name "Whalers" was chosen for the franchise in 1972 because the name contained the letters of the team's new league (the WHA) and also represented an aspect of New England's maritime heritage.

30. Zarley Zalapski's path to the big-time was something out of the ordinary, in that he played neither major junior, college nor minor league hockey before making his NHL debut. Zalapski joined the Canadian Olympic program at age 17 (1985) and was drafted by the Penguins in 1986. He entered the NHL after competing in the 1988 Winter Olympics.

31. Defenseman Neil Sheehy was the only player in Whalers' history to wear number 0.

32. Rogie Vachon was the first Kings player to have his jersey number (30) retired.

33. Victor Nechaev became the first Soviet-trained player to score an NHL goal when he tallied against the New York Rangers during a 5-3 Kings win on October 17, 1982.

34. It is believed that Wayne Gretzky has autographed only one copy of his 1988 Topps hockey card (his first as a King). The Great One is said to be saving the card for his daughter, Paulina.

35. Two North Stars have won the Calder Memorial Trophy as the NHL's top rookie: Bobby Smith (1979) and Danny Grant (1969).

36. Minnesota native Jon Casey, goaltending luminary for the North Stars, won a Minnesota state championship at Grand Rapids High School (1980) and an NCAA crown at North Dakota (1982).

37. Tim Young was the only North Star to score five goals in one game, accomplishing the feat against the New York Rangers during an 8-1 win on January 15, 1979.

38. North Star center Dave Gagner is a co-holder for most playoff points in a period, notching two goals and four points in the first period of Minnesota's 6-5 loss to Chicago in game three of the 1991 Norris Division semi-final.

39. Steve Christoff, former North Star and 1980 US Olympic team member, was the model for the Hobey Baker Award, presented annually to the nation's best college hockey player.

40. The 1918-19 Stanley Cup Championship series between Montreal and Seattle was cancelled because of an influenza epidemic.

41. Howie Morenz, known as the "Stratford Streak," severely fractured his leg during a 1937 game and died six weeks later because of complications resulting from his injury. Twenty-five thousand people filed past his casket during the memorial service held at the Montreal Forum.

42. Dr. David A. Hart, who donated the trophy awarded to the NHL's Most Valuable Player each season, never played in the NHL. However, his son Cecil led the Canadiens to a pair of championships in 10 years as their coach.

43. Goaltender Georges Vezina, also known as the Chicoutimi Cucumber for his hometown and coolness under pressure, played in 328 straight regular season games for Montreal before falling ill during a game on November 28, 1925. He was diagnosed as having turberculosis and died on March 26, 1926 at the age of 39.

He's best known as the architect of the five time Stanley Cup champion Edmonton Oilers. Opponents remember Glen "Slats" Sather as one huge pain in the neck.

44. New Jersey fans voted for the name "Devils." Runners-up were Blades, Meadowlanders and Americans.

45. Right wing John MacLean once had three hat tricks in eight days, scoring three goals in games on December 7, 9 and 15, 1988. The first two efforts made him the only Devil ever to post back-to-back three-goal games.

46. Devils president and general manager Lou Lamoriello was the driving force behind the creation of Hockey East, a college hockey conference created by five former ECAC schools (Lamoriello was serving as athletic director for Providence College at the time). In recognition of his pioneering work, Hockey East (which later grew to eight teams) voted in 1988 to name the league championship trophy the Lamoriello Cup.

47. Mike Bossy is one of two players (Wayne Gretzky being the other) to score his 500th goal into an empty net.

48. Bossy holds the NHL record for goals by a rookie, scoring 53 in 1977-78.

49. The Islanders were the first NHL team to be invited to the White House, earning an invitation from President Ronald Reagan following their 1983 Stanley Cup victory.

50. Derek King set an Islander record for three fastest goals on October 15, 1991, notching a hat trick in 78 seconds during the first period of a 7-6 overtime loss to the Penguins.

51. Mike Gartner is the only player to have scored his 500th NHL goal in a Ranger uniform.

52. Alexei Kovalev, the Rangers' top Entry Draft choice in 1991, is the first Soviet player to be chosen in the first round of the draft.

53. Dudley "Red" Garrett, who played for the Rangers in 1943, was the first NHL player to die in action during World War II. The American Hockey League's Rookie of the Year award is named in Garrett's honor.

54. Madison Square Garden is not in Madison Square — but it was

when first built in 1879. The current building is the fourth to carry the title Madison Square Garden.

55. Rod Gilbert, the Rangers' all-time leader in goals, assists and points, scored 406 goals and 1,021 points during his 16-year NHL career. Gilbert almost didn't make the NHL, nearly losing his left leg during two operations to correct damage done to his back (which was broken during a junior game).

56. Ron Hextall is the only goaltender in NHL history to shoot and score a goal, a feat he has accomplished twice.

57. Bobby Clarke was the first skater from an expansion team to win the Hart Memorial Trophy as the NHL's Most Valuable Player, capturing the award in 1975.

58. When the Flyers felt the need for a little extra bit of luck, they used to play a recording of Kate Smith's rendition of "God Bless America" instead of the national anthem. Philadelphia once compiled an incredible record of 60-13-3 when "God Bless America" was performed before games.

59. Reg Leach is the only Flyer in history to score five goals in a game, accomplishing the feat May 6, 1976 against Boston. Leach is also the only player in franchise history to score 60 goals in a season.

60. The Flyers hold the longest undefeated streak in all of professional sports, going 25-0-10 from October 14, 1979 through January 6, 1980. A 7-1 loss to Minnesota ended the streak, but then the Flyers ripped off another 13-game undefeated streak.

61. The Penguins play at Pittsburgh's Civic Arena (also known as "The Igloo"), which features the largest retractable roof in the country. The arena was originally designed for use by the Civic Light Opera company.

62. The triangle on the old Penguins logo represents Pittsburgh's "Golden Triangle" where the Ohio, Allegheny and Monongahela Rivers meet.

63. Mario Lemieux is the only player in NHL history to have scored

five goals in each of five possible ways in one game. In a December 31, 1988 game against the Devils, Lemieux scored at even-strength, shorthanded, on the power play, on a penalty shot and into an empty net.

64. Defenseman Jim Paek is the only Korean-born player in NHL history.

65. Penguins general manager Craig Patrick is the fifth member of the Patrick family to have his name inscribed on the Stanley Cup, joining grandfather Lester, grand-uncle Frank, father Lynn, and uncle Muzz as a Cup-winner.

66. Nordique is a French word which means "people from the north."

67. The Quebec Colisée was built in 1930, but the first hockey game was not played until 12 years later. A 1949 fire destroyed the arena prompting the city to build a new 10,000-seat Colisée. The building was renovated and modernized in 1980 to its current status.

68. Mats Sundin was the first European player to be selected first overall when Quebec chose him in the 1989 Entry Draft.

69. Jean-Claude Tremblay was the first NHL player to sign with the Nordiques, then a World Hockey Association franchise, on July 20, 1972. The same day Maurice Richard was hired as the team's first head coach.

70. Guy Lafleur, who finished his illustrious playing career with the Nords, is only the second player in history to play in the NHL after gaining Hall of Fame status. Gordie Howe was the first.

71. After San Jose was granted an NHL franchise, a contest was held to name the new team. From the more than 5,700 entries received from fans, one of the finalists was "Icehawks," but the monicker was finally rejected because of the potential for being confused with Blackhawks. Of course, no one was actually going to confuse the new team's playing caliber with that of Chicago — at least not for years to come!

72. Winger Craig Coxe scored the first goal in Sharks history, tallying at 4:09 of the third period during San Jose's opening night 4-3 loss at Vancouver.

73. Pat Falloon, a right winger, is the first Entry Draft choice in Sharks' history.

74. In the late fall of 1990 — nearly a year before they actually began play — the Sharks took the interest earned from their early season ticket sales and bought more than 500 turkeys to give to needy families in the Santa Cruz area, many of whom had been hard hit by the severe earthquake that had interrupted that year's World Series.

75. The first Sharks team, few games though it might win, boasted two NHL award winners on its initial roster: goalie Brian Hayward had won the Jennings Trophy for lowest goals-against for three consecutive seasons as a Montreal Canadien (1987, '88 and '89), while veteran defenseman Doug Wilson had earned the Norris Trophy as the league's best defenseman in 1982 while playing for the Blackhawks.

76. Red Berenson holds the NHL record for goals in a road game, scoring six against Doug Favell and the Philadelphia Flyers on November 7, 1968, while playing for the St. Louis Blues. Red almost scored a seventh, but hit the post instead.

77. Simply proving that they were the best of a bad new lot (coached by a man — Scotty Bowman — who would one day be recognized known as one of the greatest coaches ever to grace the NHL), the St. Louis Blues managed to gain the Stanley Cup finals each of their first three seasons (1968, '69 and '70).

78. The St. Louis Arena was originally dedicated on September 24, 1929, as a permanent home for the National Dairy Show!

79. Connie Madigan became the oldest rookie in NHL history when he was summoned from the minors by the Blues at age 38, in 1973.

80. In 1990-91 Blues right winger Brett Hull became only the third player in NHL history to score 50 goals in fewer than 50 games.

81. The St. Louis entry into the NHL was named the Blues in honor of the city's famous musical tradition.

82. When the NHL was created in 1917, the Toronto franchise was tabbed the Arenas. In 1919 the name was changed to St. Patricks, or St. Pats, and in 1926 they gained their present-day name of Maple Leafs.

83. Former Leaf hero Darryl Sittler leads the Leafs in goals (389) and points (916), while also holding the NHL's single-game scoring record of 10 points (six goals and four assists).

84. The Leafs' famed "Kid Line" of Charlie Conacher, Joe Primeau and Busher Jackson was formed during the 1929-30 season — basically the first of the great NHL trios. The trio had its greatest season during 1931-32, when its members finished 1-2-4 in league scoring, respectively.

85. The great Syl Apps, captain of the Maple Leafs during the 1940s, competed for Canada in the 1936 Olympics, finishing sixth in the pole vault event.

86. Claude Provost, who won the first of his nine Stanley Cup titles in 1959 is the only player to have won that many championships but not be inducted into the Hall of Fame.

87. Defenseman Borje Salming is generally credited as the first European-trained impact player in the NHL. He played 17 seasons for Toronto, was a six-time all-star and is the Leafs' career assist leader.

88. The Canadian Broadcasting Corporation created the first hockey telecast in Canadian history on March 21, 1951 by broadcasting pictures of the Maple Leafs-Canadiens game to a control room inside Maple Leaf Gardens.

89. Toronto's game against Montreal, January 21, 1936, was post-poned as a show of respect for King George V, who had died the previous day. The memorial was the first of its kind in league history.

90. The late Babe Pratt, a long-time executive with the Canucks, a

two-time Stanley Cup winner and once the winner of the Hart Memorial Trophy as the NHL's Most Valuable Player, was also a player in the only scoreless, penalty-less tie in NHL history. The game was played on February 20, 1944, between Chicago and Toronto. Pratt played for Toronto and won his Hart Trophy at the end of that season.

91. Bud Poile, Vancouver's first general manager, was also the first general manager of the Philadelphia Flyers and by remarkable coincidence also played — as did Pratt — in that 1944 scoreless, penalty-less game.

92. Stan Smyl holds the Vancouver career franchise records for games played, goals, assists and points.

93. Trevor Linden, who set a club record for goals by a rookie, with 30 in 1988-89, is the youngest Canuck to have scored 100 career NHL points.

94. Vancouver's first shutout is also the only 0-0 tie the club has played in its history. The Canucks skated to a 0-0 tie against Toronto on October 27, 1971. Dunc Wilson, in goal for Vancouver, faced Bernie Parent.

95. Defenseman Rod Langway was the first American player (even though he was actually born in Maaq, Taiwan!) to win the Norris Trophy, capturing the award for the first time in 1983. He is also the only Cap to play in every Washington playoff series, through 1992.

96. Dennis Maruk is the only Cap to score 60 goals in a season (1981-82).

97. Bengt Gustafsson is the only Capital to score five goals in one game (January 18, 1984, at Philadelphia).

98. Washington center Demitri Khristich was the youngest player to be released for NHL play by the Soviet Ice Hockey Federation.

99. Lars-Erik Sjoberg and Thomas Steen became the first and second Swedish hockey players respectively ever to captain an NHL hockey team. Interestingly, each was tapped for this honour while playing with the Winnipeg Jets.

100. The Winnipeg Jets retired Bobby Hull's #9 in 1989, making him only the second player (Gordie Howe — Detroit and Hartford) in NHL history to have his number retired by two teams. Chicago also retired Hull's number.

What breed of duck is as extinct as the Dodo bird? Why it's none other than the Long Island Ducks Hockey Club, formerly of the old Eastern League. The captain here in 1965 is Eddie Stankiewicz.

THE ALL-TIME LIST OF HOCKEY NICKNAMES

Sid Abel, Detroit, Chicago = *Ole Bootnose*
Clarence John Abel, Rangers, Chicago = *Taffy*
Keith Acton, Philadelphia, Edmonton, North Stars, Canadiens =
    Woody
Keith Allen, Detroit = *Bingo*
Viv Allen, Americans = *Squee*
Glenn Anderson, Edmonton, Toronto = *Andy*
Ron Anderson, Detroit, Los Angeles, St. Louis, Buffalo =
    Goings
Tom Anderson, Detroit, Americans = *Cowboy*
George Armstrong, Toronto = *The Chief*
Bob Ash, Winnipeg, Indianapolis (WHA) = *Squeaky*
Don Ashby, Toronto, Colorado, Edmonton = *Ash*
Walt Atanas, Rangers = *Ants*
Irvine Bailey, Toronto = *Ace*
Ken Baumgartner, Kings, Islanders, Toronto = *Bomber*
Frank Beaton, Cincinnatti, Edmonton, Birmingham (WHA), Rangers
    = *Seldom*
Barry Beck, Colorado, Rangers, Los Angeles = Bubba
Jean Beliveau, Montreal = *Le Gros Bill*
Jim Benzelock, Atlanta, Chicago, Quebec (WHA) = *The Big Cat*
Red Berenson, Montreal, Rangers, St. Louis, Detroit = *The Red Baron*
Craig Berube, Philadelphia, Edmonton, Toronto, Flames = *Chief*
Tom Bladon, Philadelphia, Pittsburgh, Edmonton, Winnipeg, De-
    troit = *Bomber*
Mike Blaisdell, Detroit = *Blazer*
Hector Blake, Montreal = *Toe*
Russ Blinco, Montreal, Chicago = *Beaver*
Frank Boll, Toronto, Americans, Boston = *Buzz*
Carl Boone, Boston = *Buddy*
Mike Bossy, Islanders = *Boss*
Emile Bouchard, Montreal = *Butch*
Frank Boucher, Ottawa, Rangers = *Raffles*
Bob Bourne, Islanders, Los Angeles = *Bournie*
Bob Boyd, Rangers, Americans = *Boydie*
Irwin Boyd, Boston, Detroit = *Yank*
Ralph Buchanan, Rangers = *Bucky*
John Bucyk, Detroit, Boston = *Chief*
Hyman Buller, Detroit, Rangers = *The Blueline Blaster*
Pavel Bure, Canucks = *Russian Rocket*

Jerry Butler, Rangers, St. Louis, Toronto, Vancouver = *Bugsy*
Lyndon Byers, Bruins = *L.B.*
Larry Cahan, Toronto, Rangers, Oakland, Los Angeles, Chicago = *Hank*
Jim Cain, Montreal, Toronto = *Dutch*
Brett Callighen, New England (WHA), Edmonton = *Key*
Colin Campbell, Vancouver, Pittsburgh, Colorado, Edmonton, Detroit = *Soupy*
Jack Carlson, Minnesota, Edmonton, New England (WHA), St. Louis = *The Big Bopper*
Bob Carpenter, Bruins, Kings, Rangers, Capitals = *Carpy B*
Al Carr, Toronto = *Red*
Gerry Carson, Montreal, Rangers = *Stub*
Bill Chalmers, Rangers = *Chick*
Don Cherry, Boston = *Grapes*
Ron Chipperfield, Vancouver, Calgary, Edmonton, Quebec (WHA) = *The Magnificent 7*
Keith Christiansen, Minnesota = *Huffer*
Jeff Chychrun, Philadelphia, Kings, Penguins = *Chych*
Francis Clancy, Ottawa, Toronto = *King*
Aubrey Clapper, Boston = *Dit*
Norm Collings, Montreal = *Dodger*
Charlie Conacher, Toronto, Detroit, Americans = *The Bomber*
Hugh Conn, Americans = *Red*
Yvan Cournoyer, Montreal = *The Roadrunner*
Rosie Couture, Chicago, Montreal = *Lolo*
Floyd Curry, Montreal = *Busher*
Hank Damore, Rangers = *Lou Costello*
Dan Daoust, Montreal, Toronto = *Dangerous*
Harry Darragh, Piitsburgh, Philadelphia, Boston = *Howl*
Bob Davie, Boston = *Pinkie*
Clarence Day, Toronto, Americans = *Hap*
Ron Delorme, Colorado, Vancouver = *Chief*
Ray DiLorenzi, Vancouver, Calgary (WHA) = *The Hawk*
Marcel Dionne, Detroit, Los Angeles, Rangers = *Lou*
Tie Domi, Rangers, Maple Leafs = *Albanian Assassin*
Mike Dubois, Indianapolis, Quebec (WHA) = *Plywood*
Andre Dupont, Rangers, St. Louis, Philadelpia, Quebec = *Moose*
Viteslav Duris, Toronto = *Slava*
Pat Egan, Americans, Boston, Detroit, Rangers = *Boxcar*
Todd Ewen, Canadiens, St.Louis = *Animal*
Bill Fairburn, Rangers, Minnesota, St. Louis = *Magnet*

Walt Farrant, Chicago = *Whitey*
Bill Flett, Los Angeles, Philadelphia, Toronto, Atlanta, Edmonton =
    Cowboy
Robbie Ftorek, Detroit, Phoenix, Cincinatti (WHA), Quebec, Rangers
    = *Britz*
Link Gaetz, North Stars, Sharks = *Missing Link*
Johnny Gagnon, Montreal, Boston, Americans = *The Black Cat*
Garry Galley, Flyers, Bruins, Capitals, Kings = *Ga Ga*
Curt Giles, Minnesota, Rangers = *Pengy*
Clark Gillies, Islanders = *Jethro*
Brian Glenwright, Chicago, Los Angeles (WHA) = *Wimpy*
Robert Goring, Los Angeles, Islanders = *Butch*
Wilf Green, Hamilton, Americans = *Shorty*
Wayne Gretzky, Indianapolis (WHA), Edmonton, Los Angeles = *The
    Great One*
Stu Grimson, Blackhawks = *Grim Reaper*
Lloyd Gronsdahl, Boston = *Gabby*
Joe Hall, Montreal = *Bad Joe*
Doug Halward, Boston, Los Angeles, Vancouver = *Hawk*
Herb Hamel, Toronto = *Hap*
Robert Hamill, Boston, Chicago = *Red*
Joe Hardy, Oakland, California, Cleveland, Chicago, Indianapolis,
    San Diego (WHA) = *Gypsy Joe*
Jim Hargreaves, Vancouver, Winnipeg, Indianapolis, San Diego
    (WHA) = *Cement-Head*
Wilfred Hart, Detroit, Montreal = *Gizzy*
Billy Hay, Chicago = *Red*
Jim Hay, Detroit = *Red-Eye*
Fern Headley, Boston, Montreal = *Curley*
Murray Henderson, Boston = *Moe*
Camille Henry, Rangers, Chicago, St. Louis = *The Eel*
Pat Hickey, Toronto, Rangers, Colorado, Quebec = *Hitch*
Mel Hill, Boston, Americans, Toronto = *Sudden Death*
Ed Hospodar, Rangers, Hartford, Philadelphia = *Boxcar*
Bobby Hull, Chicago, Winnepeg (WHA), Hartford = *The Golden Jet*
Brett Hull, Calgary, St. louis = *The Golden Brett*
Fred Hunt, Americans, Rangers = *Fritz*
Johnny Ingoldsby, Toronto = *Ding*
Ivan Irwin, Montreal, Rangers = *Ivan the Terrible*
Walter Jackson, Americans = *Red*
Jim Jarvis, Pittsburgh, Philadelphia, Toronto = *Bud*
Rosario Joanette, Montreal = *Kitoute*

Ching Johnson, Rangers, Americans = *Ching-A-Ling Chinaman*
Bill Juzda, Rangers, Toronto = *The Fireman or The Beast*
Alex Kaleta = *Killer*
Frank Kane, Detroit = *Red*
John Keating, Detroit = *Red*
Bob Kelly, St. Louis, Pittsburgh, Chicago = *Battleship*
Bob Kelly, Philadelphia, Washington = *Mad Dog*
Ted Kennedy, Toronto = *Teeder*
Jim Klein, Boston, Americans = *Dede*
Joe Klukay, Toronto, Boston = *Duke of Paducah*
Keith Kokkola, Chicago, Birmingham = *Bear*
Jerry Korab, Chicago, Vancouver, Buffalo, Los Angeles = *Kong*
Gord Kuhn, Americans = *Doggie*
Adolph Kukulowicz, Rangers = *Aggie*
Norm Lacombe, Oilers, Philadelphia, Buffalo = *Gorilla*
Guy Lafleur, Montreal, Rangers, Quebec = *The Flower*
Dave Langevin, Edmonton (WHA), Islanders = *The Bammer*
Al Langlois, Montreal, Rangers, Detroit, Boston = *Junior*
Ben LaPrairie, Chicago = *Bun*
Pierre Larouche, Pittsburgh, Montreal, Hatrford, Rangers = *Lucky Pierre*
Jeff Lazaro, Bruins, Bruins = *Lazar*
Reggie Leach, Boston, California, Philadelphia, Detroit = *Rifle*
Albert Leduc, Montreal, Ottawa, Rangers = *Battleship*
Rejean Lemelin, Atlanta, Calgary, Bruins = *Reggie*
Mario Lemieux, Pittsburgh = *Le Magnifique*
Tony Leswick, Rangers, Detroit, Chicago, Detroit = *Tough Tony*
Don Lever, Vancouver, Atlanta, Calgary, Colorado, New Jersey = *Cleaver*
Alex Levinsky, Toronto, Rangers, Chicago = *Mine Boy*
Willy Lindstrom, Winnipeg, Edmonton = *Willy the Wisp*
Ken Linseman = *The Rat*
Norm Lowe, Rangers = *Odie*
Calum McKay, Detroit, Montreal = *Baldy*
Frank Mahovlich, Toronto, Detroit, Montreal, Birmingham (WHA) = *Big M*
Pete Mahovlich, Detroit, Montreal, Pittsburgh = *Little M*
Merlin Malinowski, Colorado, New Jersey, Hartford = *Magician*
Hector Marini, Islanders, New Jersey = *The Wrecker*
Nevin Markwart, Bruins, Flames = *The Kid*
Gilles Marotte, Boston, Chicago, Los Angeles, Rangers, St. Louis, Cincinnati, Indianapolis (WHA) = *Captain Crunch*

Eddie Mazur, Montreal, Chicago = *Spider*
Tom McCarthy, Minnesota = *Jug*
John McCormack, Toronto, Montreal, Chicago = *Goose*
Charley McVeigh, Chicago, Americans = *Rabbit*
Wayne Merrick, St. Louis, California, Cleveland, Islanders = *Bones*
Mark Messier, Indianapolis, Cincinnatti (WHA), Edmonton, Rangers = *Mess*
Rick Middleton, Rangers, Boston = *Slick*
Stan Mikita, Chicago = *Stosh*
Andy Moog, Edmonton, Bruins = *Mooger*
Howie Morenz, Montreal, Chicago, Rangers = *Stratford Streak*
Lou Nanne, Minnesota = *Sweet Lou from the Soo*
Vaclav Nedomansky, Toronto (WHA), Birmingham (WHA), Detroit, Rangers, St. Louis = *Big Ned*
Jim Neilson, Rangers, California, Cleveland, Edmonton (WHA) = *Chief*
Frank Nighbor, Ottawa, Toronto = *Dutch*
Chris Nilan, Canadiens, Rangers, Bruins = *Knuckles*
Herbert William O'Connor, Montreal, Rangers = *Buddy*
Gerry Odrowski, Detroit, Oakland, California, St. Louis, Los Angeles (WHA), Pheonix (WHA), Minnesota (WHA), Winnipeg (WHA) = *Snowy , the Hook*
John O'Flaherty, Americans = *Peanuts*
Donald Edwin O'Hearn, Ft. Worth (USHL), Springfield (AHL), Oakland (PCHL), Springfield (PCHL), Portland (PCHL), Syracuse (AHL) = *Nipper*
Jim O'Neill, Boston, Montreal = *Peggy*
Tom O'Neill, Toronto = *Windy*
Mark Osborne, Detroit, Rangers = *Ozzie*
Fredrick Murray Patrick, Rangers = *Muzz*
Lester Patrick, Rangers = *The Silver Fox*
Arthur Paul, Detroit = *Butch*
Mark Pavelich, Rangers = *Pav*
Marty Nicholas Pavelich, Detroit = *Blackie*
Gene Peacosh, New York (WHA), New Jersey (WHA), San Diego (WHA), Edmonton (WHA), Indianapolis (WHA) = *Peco*
Jim Peplinski, Calgary = *Pep*
Stefan Persson, Islanders = *Steff*
Eric Pettinger, Boston, Toronto, Ottawa = *Cowboy*
Didier Pitre, Ottawa (FAHL), Montreal (ECAHA), Montreal (NHA), Vancouver (PCHA), Montreal = *Cannonball*
Norman Robert Poile, Toronto, Chicago, Detroit, Rangers, Boston = *Bud*

Larry Popein, Rangers, Oakland = *Pope*

Jan Popiel, Chicago (WHA), Denver-Ottawa (WHA), Houston (WHA), Pheonix (WHA) = *Pope, Poper*

Walter Pratt, Rangers, Toronto, Boston = *Babe*

Rich Preston, Houston (WHA), Winnipeg (WHA), Chicago = *Cool Hand Luke*

Pat Price, Vancouver (WHA), Islanders, Edmonton, Pittsburgh, Quebec = *Pricey*

Dick Proceviat, Chicago (WHA), Indianapolis (WHA) = *Pro, Herman, Goodyear*

George Prodgers, Waterloo (OPHL), Quebec (NHA), Victoria (PCHA), Montreal Wanderers (NHA), Montreal Canadiens (NHA), Montreal 228th Battn. (NHA), Toronto, Hamilton = *Goldie*

Joel Quenneville, Toronto, Colorado, New Jersey, Hartford = *Herbie*

Don Raleigh, Rangers = *Bones*

Craig Ramsay, Buffalo = *Rammer*

Ed Reigle, Boston = *Rags*

Henri Richard, Montreal = *The Pocket Rocket*

Maurice Richard, Montreal = *The Rocket*

Howard Riopelle, Montreal = *Rip*

Elwin Romnes, Chicago, Toronto, Americans = *Doc*

Erskine Ronan, Ottawa = *Skene*

Reijo Ruotsalainen, Rangers, Edmonton, New Jersey = *Rexie, Ray, Double R, Ho*

Terry Ruskowski, Houston (WHA), Winnipeg (WHA), Chicago, Los Angeles = *Roscoe*

Vladimir Ruzicka, Oilers, Bruins = *Rosie*

Larry Sacharuk, Rangers, St. Louis, Indianapolis (WHA) = *Satch*

Don Saleski, Philadelphia, Colorado = *Big Bird*

Borje Salming, Toronto = *B.J.*

Derek Sanderson, Boston, Philadelphia, Rangers, St. Louis, Vancouver, Pittsburgh = *Turk*

Ed Sandford, Boston, Detroit, Chicago = *Sandy*

Gary Sargent, Los Angeles, Minnesota = *Sarge*

Glen Sather, Boston, Pittsburgh, Rangers, St. Louis, Montreal, Minnesota, Edmonton (WHA) = *Slats*

Jean Sauve, Buffalo = *Frankie*

Serge Savard, Montreal, Winnipeg = *The Senator*

Jim Schoenfeld, Buffalo, Detroit = *Schony*

David Schriner, Americans, Toronto = *Sweeney*

Dave Schultz, Philadelphia, Los Angeles, Pittsburgh, Buffalo = *The Hammer*

Al Secord, Boston, Chicago = *Big Al*
Rod Seiling, Toronto, Rangers, Washington, St. Louis, Atlanta = *Sod*
Dave Semenko, Edmonton (WHA), Edmonton = *Sam*
Eddie Shack, Rangers, Toronto, Boston, Los Angeles, Buffalo, Pittsburgh = *The Entertainer*
Fred Shero, Rangers = *The Fog*
Sam Hamilton Shore, Ottawa = *Hamby*
Albert Siebert, Montreal Maroons, Rangers, Boston, Montreal Canadiens = *Babe*
Risto Siltanen, Edmonton (WHA), Edmonton, Hartford = *Incredible Hulk*
Charlie Simmer, California, Cleveland, Los Angeles = *Chaz*
Joe Simpson, Americans = *Bullet*
Lars Sjoberg, Winnipeg (WHA), Winnipeg = *The Shoe, Little General*
Al Smith, Toronto, Pittsburgh, Detroit, New England (WHA) = *Smitty*
Brad Smith, Vancouver, Atlanta, Calgary, Detroit = *Smitty*
Clint Smith, Rangers, Chicago = *Snuffy*
Dalton Smith, Americans, Detroit = *Nakina*
Reginald Joseph Smith, Ottawa, Montreal, Boston, Americans = *Hooley*
Stan Smyl, Vancouver = *Steamer*
Greg Smyth, Nordiques, Philadelphia, Flames = *Smitty*
Brian Spencer, Toronto, Islanders, Buffalo, Pittsburgh = *Spinner*
Pat Stapleton, Boston, Chicago, Chicago (WHA) = *Whitey*
Pete Stemkowski, Toronto, Detroit, Rangers, Los Angeles = *Stemmer*
John Stewart, Detroit, Chicago = *Black Jack*
Nelson Stewart, Montreal, Boston, Americans = *Old Poison*
Blaine Stoughton, Pittsburgh, Toronto, Cincinnati (WHA), Indianapolis (WHA), New England (WHA), Hartford = *Stash*
Billy Stuart, Toronto, Boston = *Red*
Frank Sullivan, Toronto, Chicago = *Sully*
George Sullivan, Boston, Chicago, Rangers = *Red*
Pete Sullivan, Winnipeg (WHA), Winnipeg = *Silky*
Bobby Taylor, Philadelphia, Penguins = *Chief*
Fred Taylor, Ottawa (ECAHA, ECHA), Renfrew (NHA), Vancouver (PCHL) = *Cyclone*
Victor Teal, Islanders = *Skeeter*
Cecil Thompson, Boston, Detroit = *Tiny*
Mike Toal, Edmonton = *Toaler*
Rick Tocchet, Philadelphia, Penguins = *Toc*
Jerry Toppazzini, Boston, Chicago, Detroit = *Topper*

Zellio Toppazzini, Boston, Rangers, Chicago = *Topper*

Bryan Trottier, Islanders, Pittsburgh = *Trots*

Garry Unger, Toronto, Detroit, St. Louis, Atlanta, Los Angeles, Edmonton = *Iron Man*

Carol Vadnais, Montreal, California, Oakland, Boston, Rangers, New Jersey = *Vad*

Eric Vail, Atlanta, Calgary, Detroit = *Big Train*

Elmer Vasko, Chicago, Minnesota = *Moose*

Steve Vickers, Rangers = *Sarge*

Frank Waite, Rangers = *Deacon*

Mike Walton, Toronto, Boston, Minnesota (WHA), Vancouver, St. Louis, Chicago = *Shakey*

Grant David Warwick, Rangers, Boston, Montreal = *Knobby*

Bryan Watson, Montreal, Detroit, California, Pittsburgh, St. Louis, Washington, Cincinnati (WHA) = *Bugsy*

Harry Watson, Americans, Detroit, Toronto, Chicago = *Whipper*

Jim Watson, Detroit, Buffalo, Los Angeles (WHA), Chicago (WHA), Quebec (WHA) = *Watty*

John Webster, Rangers = *Chick*

Ralph Weiland, Boston, Ottawa, Detroit = *Cooney*

Stan Weir, California, Toronto, Edmonton (WHA), Edmonton, Colorado, Detroit = *Stash*

John Wensink, St. Louis, Boston, Quebec, Colorado, New Jersey = *Wire*

Harry Westwick, Ottawa Silver Seven = *Rat*

Juha Widing, Rangers, Los Angeles, Cleveland, Edmonton (WHA) = *Whitey*

Jim Wiemer, Rangers, Kings, Boston = *Ripper*

Dave Williams, Kings, Whalers, Canucks, Maple Leafs = *Tiger*

Carol Wilson, Toronto, Montreal, Hamilton, Chicago = *Cully*

Johnny Wilson, Detroit, Chicago, Toronto, Rangers = *The Iron Man*

Paul Woods, Detroit = *Woodsy*

Lorne Worsley, Rangers, Montreal, Minnesota = *Gump*

Stephen Wojciechowski, Detroit = *Wochy*

Roy Worters, Pittsburgh, Montreal, Americans = *Shrimp*

William Wylie, Rangers = *Wiggie*

Tim Young, Minnesota = *Blade*

Rod Zaine, Pittsburgh, Buffalo, Chicago = *Zainer*

Larry Zeidel, Detroit, Chicago, Philadelphia = *The Rock*

GOALIE NICKNAMES

Hank Bassen, Chicago, Detroit, Pittsburgh = *Red*

Johnny Bower, Rangers, Toronto = *China Wall*

Frankie Brimsek, Boston, Chicago = *Mr. Zero*

Richard Brodeur, Quebec (WHA), Islanders, Vancouver = *King Richard*

Steve Buzinski, Rangers = *The Puck Goes Inski*

Gerry Cheevers, Toronto, Boston, Cleveland (WHA) = *Cheesey*

Tony Esposito, Montreal, Chicago = *Tony O*

Emile Francis, Chicago, Rangers = *The Cat*

Gilles Gratton, Ottawa (WHA), Toronto (WHA), St. Louis, Rangers = *Gratoony the Loony*

Chris Grigg, Denver-Ottawa = *Gouler, Fig*

Glenn Hall, Detroit, Chicago, St. Louis = *Mr. Goalie*

Glen Hanlon, Vancouver, St. Louis, Rangers, Detroit = *Red*

John Henderson, Boston = *Long John*

Gord Henry, Boston = *Red*

Jim Henry, Rangers, Chicago, Boston = *Sugar Jim*

Michel Larocque, Montreal, Toronto, Philadelphia = *Bunny*

Howie Lockhart, Toronto, Quebec, Hamilton, Boston = *Holes*

Harry Lumley, Detroit, Rangers, Chicago, Toronto, Boston = *Apple Cheeks , Horse Face Haryy*

Cesare Maniago, Toronto, Montreal, Rangers, Minnesota, Vancouver = *Hail Cesare*

Ken McAuley, Rangers = *Tubby*

Frank McCool, Toronto = *Ulcers*

Mike Palmateer, Toronto, Washington = *The Popcorn Kid*

Jacques Plante, Montreal, Rangers, St. Louis, Toronto, Boston, Edmonton (WHA) = *Jake the Snake*

Chuck Rayner, Americans, Rangers = *Bonnie Prince Charlie*

Al Rollins, Toronto, Chicago, Rangers = *Ally*

Billy Smith, Los Angeles, Islanders = *The Hatchet Man*

Gary Smith, Toronto, Oakland, California, Chicago, Vancouver, Minnesota,, Washington, Indianapolis (WHA), Winnipeg (WHA), Winnipeg = *Suitcase*

Doug Soetaert, Rangers, Winnipeg = *Soapy*

Georges Vezina, Montreal = *The Chicoutimi Cucumber*

John Vanbiesbrouck, Rangers = *Beezer*

COACH NICKNAMES

Keith Allen, Philadelphia = *Bingo*
Red Berenson, St. Louis = *The Red Baron*
Frank Boucher, Rangers = *Raffles*
Don Cherry, Boston, Colorado = *Grapes*
John Ferguson, Rangers = *Fergie*
Bernie Geoffrion, Rangers, Atlanta, Montreal = *Boom Boom*
Wilf Green, Americans = *Shorty*
Alfred Lepine, Montreal = *Pit*
Joe Simpson, Americans = *Bullet*
Bob Johnson, Calgary, Pittsburgh = *Badger*
Paul Holmgren, Phildelphia, North Stars = *Homer*

"Dog" is a term used for lousy hockey players. Here's it's applied to a good one
— Cliff ("Fido") Purpur of the Chicago Blackhawks.

THE TWENTY BEST PLAYOFF PERFORMERS

1. *Maurice Richard*
   The Rocket's red glare was invariably more evident in the playoffs than at any time during the season.

2. *Henri Richard*
   When anyone asks who has been on more Stanley Cup-winning teams than anyone else, almost no one thinks of the Rocket's baby brother, Henri — the "Pocket Rocket." And yet, Henri played for 11 Montreal winners in his two decades with Les Habitants. Furthermore, this petit centerman was 37 years old when he scored 10 points (including six goals) in 17 games when he made his last Cup-winning appearance for the Canadiens in 1973 (although he would play with the team for two more seasons, including playoffs; but the Habs couldn't bring an even dozen Cup rings to the Pocket!)

3. *Gordie Howe*
   Some have disparaged Howe for his failure to score big goals during the Stanley Cup rounds, but Gordie was the leading playoff scorer no less than six times in his career.

4. *Dickie Moore*
   Twice the leading playoff scorer, Moore had his last hurrah with the St. Louis Blues after twice retiring and, despite gimpy legs, still produced an astonishing seven goals and seven assists in 18 games.

5. *Jacques Plante*
   There never would have been a Canadiens' playoff dynasty without the peerless goalkeeping of Plante. He produced the best goals against average from the 1956 playoff through the 1960 round.

6. *Jean Beliveau*
   Right behind Henri Richard in number of Stanley Cups won is Le Gros Jean, Jean Beliveau, whose name appears on Lord Stanley's silverware no less than 10 times. Beliveau was awarded the Conn Smythe Trophy in 1964-64, as he won his sixth Cup, yet he scored his greatest number of individual playoff points — 22 (six goals and 16 assists) in 1971, the last Cup Beliveau helped Montreal win, and the year he retired.

7. *Bobby Orr*
   The Bruins' extraordinary defenseman scored the Cup-winning goal in the 1970 clincher against St. Louis and was equally dominating for Boston when the Bruins won the Cup again in 1972.

8. *Ted Kennedy*
   When the Maple Leafs were in a jam during the halcyon years of the late 1940s, Kennedy could be counted on to produce the big play. He played on five Stanley Cup winners.

9. *Nels Stewart*
   When the Montreal Maroons won the Stanley Cup in 1926, Stewart scored six goals. No other player scored more than one. "Ole Poison" always was a threat in the post-season tourney.

10. *Billy Smith*
    An aggressive netminder whose toughness and heart were as remarkable as his skills, Smitty was as good a reason as any why the Islanders were able to win four straight Stanley Cups during the early 1980s. His effort against the high-scoring Oilers in 1983 was nothing short of miraculous.

11. *Syl Apps*
    The stalwart Maple Leafs captain was chiefly responsible for the ultimate playoff comeback — Toronto won four straight from Detroit after being down three games to none — in 1942, and led the Leafs to Cup wins in 1947 and 1948.

12. *Ken Dryden*
    This tall, bespectacled Cornell graduate appeared only six times in goal for Montreal at the end of the 1970-71 regular season, then astounded the hockey world as he played every one of the Habs' playoff games, earning the Conn Smythe for his remarkable efforts. Dryden played only eight seasons in the NHL, and his Canadiens gained six Stanley Cups during those years!

13. *Tim Horton*
    Admired for his defensive consistency throughout the Maple Leafs' Cup reign in in the early 1960s, Horton also produced a mighty offensive effort in 1962 finishing second in scoring with 16 points in 12 games as Toronto won the Cup.

14. *Wayne Gretzky*

The all-time leader in playoff points has yet to work his post-season magic in Hollywood, but there is no denying his accomplishments while winning four Cups with the Oilers in the 1980s.

15. *Bryan Trottier*

Not satisfied with winning four straight Cups with the Islanders in the 1980s, this high-scoring winger brought his skills and experience to Pittsburgh, where he started the new decade with two more championships as a Penguin.

16. *Red Kelly*

Only four NHLers have won eight Stanley Cups (the others being Yvan Cournoyer, Jacques Lemaire and Rocket Richard — all Canadiens — and only Kelly split those eight Cups evenly between two teams. The russet-maned Member of Parliament helped the Detroit Red Wings win in 1950, 1952, 1954 and 1955. After being traded to the Leafs in 1960, he then helped Toronto gain three consecutive Cups in 1962-3-4 and finally, his eighth in 1967. Significantly, Red's last Cup was also the last Cup won by the Leafs.

17. *Mike Bossy*

Often criticized for a noticeable lack of defensive play, Bossy nonetheless helped the Islanders win four straight Stanley Cups (1980-83) and tallied 85 goals and 160 points in 129 playoff games. The Boss also earned the Conn Smythe in 1982.

18. *Guy Lafleur*

A Conn Smythe winner in 1976-77, the fast-skating Flower helped the Canadiens to five Cups, tallying more than 20 points in three of those wins. One of only two players to retire, enter the Hall of Fame and then stage a comeback, Guy couldn't bring the Cup to the Rangers or the Nords before he retired a second time.

19. *Mario Lemieux*

Two straight Conn Smythe Trophies equalled The Great One's total. Though the Penguins performed heroically without Le Magnifique in 1992, eliminating the heavily favoured Rangers, there was an audible sigh of relief when the big guy returned, despite injuries to his hand and back. Nobody could dominate a single game — or series — like this guy, and he finally hushed those who questioned his heart.

20. *John Druce*
This obscure Capitals winger scored more goals in eight playoff games (14) than he did in 45 regular season games in 1989-90. He also added three assists to spearhead Washington's drive to the Wales Conference finals.

THE FIFTEEN CLUTCH SCORERS

1. *Maurice Richard*
The one shooter any coach would want on the ice in sudden death overtime would be the Rocket. His flair for the dramatic has never been matched, as his 18 game-winning playoff goals and six overtime playoff goals attest.

2. *Mel "Sudden Death" Hill*
A modest scorer for the Boston Bruins during the 1938-39 season, Hill scored a pair of sudden death goals against the Rangers early in the playoff series and the overtime winner in the seventh game.

3. *Modere "Mud" Bruneteau*
The Detroit Red Wings and Montreal Canadiens played the longest game ever on March 24, 1936. Bruneteau scored the winner for Detroit six minutes and 30 seconds after the ninth period began.

4. *Ken Doraty*
Prior to Bruneteau's classic, Toronto Maple Leafs forward Ken Doraty settled what was then the longest game ever on April 3, 1933, with a goal against Boston at 4:46 of the sixth overtime period.

5. *Howie Morenz*
The Stratford Streak was the Maurice Richard of his era and generally considered to be the hardest player in the league to stop.

6. *Frank Boucher*
Ever reliable, Boucher paced the New York Rangers to their first Stanley Cup in 1928 with the only goals in a 2-0 win over the Montreal Maroons in the decisive game.

7. *Bobby Nystrom*

   Though not a prolific scorer by any means, this rugged and determined right wing is second only to Maurice Richard in overtime playoff goals. His four tallies include the Cup-winner in 1980 against Philadelphia which signalled the arrival of the last true dynasty.

8. *Nels Stewart*

   "Ole Poison" was the man for the Montreal Maroons; a shooter of consummate accuracy whose clutch skills were underestimated.

9. *Max Bentley*

   The manifold skills of the Dipsy Doodle Dandy were amply demonstrated in 1947, 1948, 1949, 1950 and 1951 when the Toronto Maple Leafs were the class of the NHL.

10. *Mike Bossy*

    The ideal sharpshooter was no less magnificent in the playoffs as in the regular season, tallying 17 game-winning goals, second only to Richard and Wayne Gretzky, who played in more games than the Boss.

11. *Wayne Gretzky*

    After a loss in the 1983 finals to the Islanders, there was some question about his prime-time ability, which was put to rest four Cups later. Though he has been effectively shadowed and subdued in recent seasons, his accomplishments speak loudly, especially the 10 shorthanded goals.

12. *Leo Reise Jr.*

    Basically a defensive defenseman with limited scoring talents, Reise emerged as an incredible clutch shooter in the bitter and bloody 1950 Stanley Cup Semi-final between the Red Wings and the Maple Leafs. With Detroit trailing two games to one, Reise scored a sudden-death goal in the second overtime of game three. He won the series with an overtime goal in the seventh match.

13. *Mario Lemieux*

    This superstar only recently got the chance to show what he can do in late-round championship play, and he wasted no time getting in all the highlight films. His furious scoring rush in game five of the 1990-1991 final against Minnesota, and an all-out assault on Ed Belfour in the 1992 finals have already provided the foundation for a Richard-like reputation in the clutch. Only Mario — specifically his back — can stop Mario when the game, or the series, is on the line.

14. *Jari Kurri*
This Finn's playoff numbers place him in the company of teammate Wayne Gretzky, as well as the Richards and Bossys of the hockey world, though he has always been overshadowed by The Great One. A sub-par return to the NHL should not detract from his achievements in Stanley Cup play, which include seven shorthanded goals and six hat tricks.

15. *John MacLean*
Though he has yet to see his name on Lord Stanley's mug, Johhny Mac has scored enough clutch goals to give the Devils an identity, as well as their first playoff berth on a thrilling overtime tally in the 1988 season finale in Chicago. To prove it wasn't a fluke, MacLean continued to perform in clutch situations during New Jersey's trek to the semi-finals that year. He never failed New Jersey in his role as the team sharpshooter.

THE TEN BEST DEFENSIVE FORWARDS

1. *Claude Provost*
The eminently clean guardian of the likes of Bobby Hull and other big guns, Provost played on nine Montreal Canadiens' Stanley Cup winners. They couldn't have done it without him.

2. *Joe Klukay:*
Known as the Duke of Paducah, Klukay labored on the Toronto Maple Leafs' late 1940s Cup winners in the shadow of Syl Apps, et. al., but his defensive work and penalty killing were flawless.

3. *Ed Westfall*
When Bobby Orr and the Big Bad Bruins were winning Stanley Cups in 1970 and 1972, Westfall was neutralizing the enemy aces with magnificent aplomb while managing to score a few himself.

4. *Marty Pavelich*

   Complementing the Production Line on the awesome Detroit Red Wings of the 1950s was this slithering center who tormented the foe with his tenacious checking.

5. *Bob Gainey*

   The NHL struck the Frank Selke trophy for the best defensive forward in 1978, and Bob Gainey of the Montreal Canadiens won it for the next four consecutive seasons, continuing to sparkle through 1987-88.

6. *Bob Nevin*

   During the Toronto Maple Leafs' playoff winning reign of the early 1960s, Nevin's work on right wing went unheralded by the masses, but not by general manager-coach Punch Imlach.

7. *Nick Metz*

   Joe Klukay's alter ego for several years in Toronto, Metz preceded The Duke, playing on Cup winners in 1942 and 1945 before the late 1940s dynasty gave him a smidgen of prominence.

8. *Tony Leswick*

   So effective was Leswick, the New York Ranger, against Gordie Howe, that the Detroit Red Wings dealt for him to get him off Gordie's back. With Tony on their side, the Wings won three Stanley Cups.

9. *Red Kelly*

   Having been an all-star defensman, Kelly was superbly equipped to play defensive center, as he did after being dealt from the Red Wings to the Maple Leafs.

10. *Steve Kasper*

    During the 1980-81 and 1981-82 seasons, when Wayne Gretzky was breaking all existing scoring records, one center was able to effectively neutralize Gretzky. Kasper, the Boston Bruins defensive ace, was that thinking young man and was rewarded with the Frank J. Selke Trophy. By 1987-88, he added offense to his defense totalling 26 goals, 44 assists, and 70 points.

11. *Guy Carbonneau*

    This Montreal center showed smarts in both ends of the ice, even though he could probably survive on offense alone. Not a big player, he reads the ice well and uses his speed to advantage in handling opponents. He won the Selke Trophy in 1988, 1989 and 1992.

12. *Dirk Graham*

A solid 200 pounds on a five-foot, eleven-inch frame, Graham knew how to use his body, especially in the claustrophobic confines of Chicago, where he was appreciated by fans and teammates alike.

13. *Esa Tikkanen*

A Finn hated by opponents for his broken language taunts, Tikkanen was a fine defensive player who handled former teammate Wayne Gretzky as well as anyone, stifling his production in crucial playoff games.

14. *Bryan Trottier*

This sure Hall-of-Famer, built like the proverbial fire plug, used his enormous leg strength to deliver devastating bodychecks. While age slowed him down, Bryan still could deliver enough rough stuff to help the Penguins to two Cups, and this after helping the Islanders to win four in a row!

15. *Laurie Boschman*

Buried in Winnipeg for most of his long career, Boschman's skills in his own end of the rink became evident after he was traded to New Jersey. His work as a penalty killer and mostly effective shadow of Mario Lemieux in the 1990-91 playoffs deserved recognition.

Best Put-Down of a Put-Down

Mario Lemieux, after claiming his second championship for Pittsburgh in the spring of 1992, responded to an accusation by then-Chicago coach Mike Keenan that Mario embarrassed himself by "taking dives" in the series.

"I think I'll go into the dressing room right now," said Lemieux, "and dive into the Stanley Cup."

The Best late-Round Draft Picks

1. Luc Robitaille — Los Angeles - 9th round, 171st overall
2. Chris Nilan — Montreal - 21st choice, 231st overall
3. Gary Suter — Flames - 9th choice, 180 overall
4. Gord Murphy — Flyers - 10th round, 189 overall
5. Mikhail Tatarinov — Washington - 10th choice, 225 overall
6. Craig MacTavish — Bruins - 9th choice, 153rd overall
7. Sergei Makarov — Flames - 14th choice, 231st overall
8. Kelly Miller — Rangers - 9th choice, 183rd overall
9. Cliff Ronning — St. Louis - 9th choice, 134th overall
10. Brett Hull — Flames - 6th choice, 117th overall
11. Petri Skriko — Vancouver - 7th choice, 157th overall
12. Kevin Stevens — Los Angeles - 6th choice, 108th overall
13. Doug Gilmour — St. Louis - 4th choice, 134th overall

The Best Brother Acts

Boucher	—	Frank, Bill and George
Richard	—	Maurice and Henri
Patrick	—	Frank and Lester
Patrick	—	Muzz and Lynn
Bentley	—	Max, Doug and Reg
Cook	—	Bill, Bun and Bud
Hull	—	Bobby and Dennis
Esposito	—	Phil and Tony
Plager	—	Bob, Barclay and Bill
Conacher	—	Charlie, Lionel and Roy
Colville	—	Mac and Neil

Mahvolich	—	Frank and Pete
Pronovost	—	Marcel and Jean
Maloney	—	Don and Dave
Howe	—	Marty and Mark
Watson	—	Joe and Jim
Dionne	—	Marcel and Gilbert
Broten	—	Neal, Aaron and Paul
Miller	—	Kelly, Kevin and Kip

BEST ALL-TIME FREE AGENT ACQUISTIONS

1. Peter Stastny — Quebec 1980
2. Dave Poulin — Philadelphia 1983
3. Marty McSorley — Penguins 1982
4. Jamie Macoun — Calgary 1983
5. Brian MacLellan — Los Angeles 1982
6. Steve Thomas — Toronto 1984
7. Mark Tinordi — Rangers 1987
8. Steve Duchesne — Los Angeles 1984
9. Chris Dahlquist — Penguins 1985
10. Geoff Courtnall — Boston 1983
11. Dino Ciccarelli — Minnesota 1979
12. Phil Bourque — Penguins 1982
13. Joe Mullen — St. Louis 1979
14. Borje Salming — Toronto 1973
15. Ilkka Sinisalo — Phildelphia 1981
16. Brian Skrudland — Montreal 1983
17. Tim Kerr — Flyers 1979
18. Ron Flockhart — Flyers 1980
19. Greg Adams — Devils 1984
20. Jon Casey — Northstars 1984
21. Ed Belfour — Blackhawks 1987
22. Glenn Healy — Los Angeles 1985

Printed in Canada